CLASSIC GARDEN PLANS

CLASSIC GARDEN PLANS

DAVID STUART

TIMBER PRESS
Portland, Oregon

First published in North America in 2004 by
Timber Press, Inc.
The Haseltine Building
133 S.W. Second Avenue, Suite 450
Portland, Oregon 97204-3527, U.S.A.
www.timberpress.com

ISBN 0-88192-643-4

A catalog record for this book is available from the Library of Congress.

Printed and bound in Singapore by Tien Wah Press

1 2 3 4 5 6 7 8 9

*Half-title page: A gazebo in the White Garden at Sissinghurst, draped
with* Rosa mulliganii.

Title page: A cascade of white wisteria on the bridge at Giverny.

Opposite: The sumptuous flower-head of the white calla lily,
Zantedeschia aethiopica.

CONTENTS

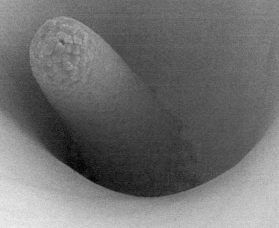

INTRODUCTION

T HIS BOOK is filled with garden plans. Designed to fit into a quite small space, each is based on some of the most romantic, marvellous, beautiful gardens in the world. Most are also gardens in the fullest sense, making use of the myriad and wonderful ways of using plants to create a delightful and fulfilling space. Many of the originals are vast schemes – dreams really – but all are dreams that are scaleable, with elements that can be used to make lovely gardens in very much smaller spaces, and with plantings that, wanting only nurture, can give abundant pleasure freely to prince or pauper, and anyone in between. They are taken from some of the great garden traditions of the temperate regions of the world, and contain some of its most lovely plants.

Here, a 'classic' garden is one that has something that is universally applicable, something that works at all sorts of levels, in the external world as well as in the heart of the gardener. Each has a plan that logically determines the gardener's movement through the space, and serves as a strong framework on which to place the planting. Each plan also has something that tries to express the garden owner's dreams of some ideal form. All the gardens on which the plans in this book have been based have different ways of doing this. But what makes them classic is their underlying power, the motive force behind the imaginative verve that led to their formation, whether this happens to be dreams of power and control, of times past or places lost, or visions of the rebuilding of some sort of vanished Eden, with no snake but plenty of sensual splendour.

Some of the gardens have been built by kings and princes, others by gardeners with much less wealth. But because they are dreams, they can also be shared and so become independent dreams in their own right. Why not have your garden filled with white azaleas and amethyst magnolias? Why not plant your garden entirely for summer nights, or as a place to show off the world's most ravishing waterlilies? Why not have a sumptuous orchard that might well fell Adam, or a garden dense with the most magical roses? Here's how!

Generosity of scale is as important in small gardens as it is in grand ones; here the rambling rose 'Bennet's Seedling' drapes a log-built pergola at Roseraie de l'Haÿ, but the same planting would make a fine boundary in a tiny garden.

As to the plans themselves, every garden is unique, in shape, in location, in topography, in outlook, in local climatic conditions. It is, of course, impossible to take all this into account, so it has seemed simplest to adopt a perfectly standard sort of garden, rectangular, without extreme changes in level, and in one of the cool temperate parts of the globe. I hope that the reader will easily be able to adapt the ideas shown for his or her own site. The fundamental plans will work anywhere, but the plantings may need adjustment when you start looking through the 'shopping lists'. Some plants may be hard to find, or not relevant to your garden. For instance, in the Artful Orchard at Ashton Wold (pages 134–141), the plans suggest apple varieties that were widely available to late-19th-century gardeners in Britain when that orchard was planted. But French or Scandinavian, or eastern Canadian or Australian gardeners had, by then, hundreds of their own apple varieties to choose from. If that's where you live, use those varieties if you can find them, or modern sorts if you can't. In other gardens, the plans suggest roses to use, using names in current use in Britain, and sometimes North America. However, the same plants may well have different names in other European countries, and almost certainly in France and Germany. Or, they may not be available at all. If something in the shopping lists can't be found, then use what is local, and what is lovely. Where there are easy alternatives that might suit, I've added some suggestions. Climate zones are some help, but in complex landscapes, local conditions can be exceptionally variable. In my present garden, a harsh winter can kill some roses, figs, mahonias, schizostylis, and more. A previous garden, only thirty miles away, gave us plentiful figs and peaches, and the thought of

This ancient gateway at William Robinson's Gravetye Manor frames the sort of herbaceous planting that he liked near the house, in contrast to the wilder style he advocated for woodland. Here, sages, artemisias, eryngiums and perovskias are grown informally in front of an old purple buddleia.

losing a rose to cold seemed entirely mysterious. On the whole, don't garden too much against your local climate. A mossy Japanese garden of contemplation is easy in a moist cool climate, but not in semi-desert. The langorous Moonlight Garden from northern India (pages 32–39) is a possibility in a London or Paris suburban or city garden, but cannot easily be achieved in Alaska.

Fitting one of the plans to your garden may not be straightforward. The designs here assume a piece of ground about 10.5–12m/35–40ft wide and about 18m/60ft long. They also assume a more or less flat site, though many of the plans would adapt splendidly to a sloping one. The plans also assume that the garden does not have much of a prospect beyond its confines, in which case a planted or built boundary both shuts out the surrounding view and concentrates the eye on the garden plan and planting. Some of the plans absolutely need enclosure to work: parterres, like the ones for the Baroque Parterre (pages 40–49) or the Moonlight Garden, need a frame in which to see them. Unframed, as they sometimes are, they lose much of their impact. In regions or in housing developments where boundaries are sometimes frowned upon, it may be easier to choose one of the 'wild' plantings favoured by Miriam Rothschild (the Artful Orchard) or William Robinson (a Copse Garden, pages 58–67). I've also assumed that the house, or living quarters, are somewhere to the south of the page, and that doorways can open easily on to paths or some sort of terrace or patio.

If your garden has an irregular shape, some of the more formal plans will be hardest to adapt. It is best to scale down the plan so that the rectangular shape is still intact, and use the garden 'offcuts' to increase the background planting. Alternatively, fill any extra space with one of the informal plans, and so have other gardens entirely, so that a Topiary Garden leads to an Artful Orchard or a hazel Copse Garden.

In any case, draw your garden on to squared paper, then draw the outlines of the plan you want to use into the space, and see how the scale compares with the

plan in the book. That will enable you to calculate, at least roughly, the plant quantities.

If your garden and the plan are fairly well matched, the quantities suggested in the plant 'shopping lists' are designed to give you a good show of herbaceous plants in the second or third season. Hedging and trees take a while longer – important elements like yew, holly and box hedges can be frustrating. Yew and holly put on perhaps a maximum of 30cm/12in a season, box about half that.

Each garden entry is split into a number of sections. The first puts the garden in an historical frame of reference, and explains in at least some measure why it is exciting, and why it is one of the garden 'classics'. Whether the garden plan page is a synthesis or a fragment of the original, 'Notes on the plan' gives some of the rationale behind the adaptation, so that it can be related clearly to the 'real' garden.

The sections on 'Building it' cover the basic framework of what is needed, especially as to design matters. However, where there are rather elaborate building works, especially the larger built elements like pavilions, rockwork, retaining walls and so on, the text gives only an outline of how to do it. You will certainly need to refer to some sort of construction manual, or get a builder or carpenter. To make the larger ponds and pools you will need some specialist help too, especially as the technology for their construction is continually improving. Though the garden's plants are mostly what makes the place attractive, romantic or productive, some of a garden's built features give the keynote to the garden look. A Monet garden is hardly Monet without a viridian green bridge; a meadow as sophisticated as those around the orchard at Ashton Wold does not have the same appeal if the mown path does not lead to a shaggy rustic pavilion. On a lesser scale, the garden's 'props' – pots, seating, urns, statuary and so on – also need consideration. The notes give some idea of what is worth trying in order to keep the look of the garden focused.

Though the book is, of course, primarily about design and much less about the technical aspects of

Opposite: Amidst the Tillandsia-draped live oaks, cherries, magnolias and azaleas of Afton Villa, the handsome statuary makes a thrilling contrast; in a small garden, nothing as grand is necessary, for a single large pot or urn can provide as much impact.

Below: Hard surfaces in the garden should be treated with as much thought and imagination as plants and planting. In the Chinese Scholar's Garden, Suzhou, and using the simplest of materials, paths and paved areas are made into exciting garden elements in their own right.

gardening, the 'Planting and maintaining it' section is the most crucial. Ways of planting hedges, increasing ferns or looking after 'old roses' are described for the gardens in which they are most important, though the techniques are also used in other gardens in the book. A number of gardens need plants grown from seed. If you are a beginner gardener, then you will need to read the seed packets carefully, and probably buy a 'how to' book. However, growing plants from seed is extremely easy; after all, it is how plants reproduce. It is also great fun, so don't be put off. A number of others, like the Moonlight Garden and the Baroque Patterre Garden, are 'bedding' gardens, and need their plants changed twice a year. Unless you consistently buy in new stock, and throw away the old, this presupposes that part of your garden is devoted to growing the material when it is not on show, or storing dormant bulbs and so on, mostly over winter. Some of the plans have lent themselves easily to this provision, but others assume a service area to the garden off-plan. One tremendously important element of maintenance and care can be stated here to avoid repeating it for every single plan: plants in the early days of a planting need help. Weeds need suppressing. Water needs to be applied whenever necessary. Pests and diseases need to be controlled. Every garden designer knows how frustrating it is to see a scheme that should have worked well falling to pieces and looking awful, because the new owners have not managed these essential tasks. Maintenance is hard work at the beginning, but becomes very much less onerous in subsequent seasons.

Great gardens can be thrilling places to be: expressive of many human desires, filled with the exquisite form of plants, the colours and textures of leaves in spring and autumn, the patter of rain falling on bamboo or on the broad leaves of banana or hosta, the sound of water falling into pools or formal tanks, the perfume of flowers – but above all the sheer extravagance that the plant world can so easily heap upon the astonished gardener.

However impossible huge vistas or ornament in marble and bronze may be for owners of tiny gardens, the plant glories are for everyone. The rest can be scaled down, or copied in more simple ways. The more enchanting a tiny space becomes, the less great avenues or views of the Atlas Mountains matter. So, here, the plans are for small spaces in which to go for the greatest effect in one aspect of the garden: maximum perfume perhaps; or to concentrate on the glories of one season – spring, or summer – or on sumptuous colours, or the sensuous delights that water can provide.

During the writing of this book, the filigree of bare branches beyond my windows here, with drifts of hellebores and a few pale pink hepaticas below, have become transformed, in my imagination, into each of these plans in turn. The pools, matted tangles of Japanese irises and duckweed, have magically become marble tanks of clearest water, romantic rock-girt depths for a troupe of lazy black and scarlet carp, or home to waterlilies that my pools are too overshadowed to grow. The old flower beds have become impeccable parterres, or have mysteriously produced elegant topiary peacocks. The apple trees, half choked with honeysuckle and clematis, have become coppiced hazels or live oaks draped with Spanish moss. All the plans have become fantasies of what perhaps could be here – the problem is choosing which one to do. I've had great fun with all of them.

Finally, as a note of comfort, if you get impatient and frustrated, even angry, because your garden has not instantly or exactly transformed itself into the romance of Giverny or the elegance of the White Garden at Sissinghurst, remember this: real gardening takes time.

In Margery Fish's garden at East Lambrook Manor, it is the seemingly artless simplicity of the planting that delights. In spring, snowdrops and hellebores shine like jewels beneath the trees.

A CHINESE SCHOLAR'S GARDEN

THE MASTER OF THE FISHING NETS, SUZHOU

THE GROUP OF MARVELLOUS GARDENS in southern China – some dating from the 15th century or even earlier, and known as the 'Scholars' Gardens' – surprise many Westerners because of their complexity and lavishness. These scholars, whilst indeed scholarly and intensely civilized, often acted as high officials to the Chinese emperors, and made substantial fortunes. In periods of disfavour, they returned to their native places, and filled their gardens with pavilions and ponds, transporting gnarled pines and even more gnarled rocks to further beautify them. One such scholar is reputed to have named his garden 'Fisherman's Retreat' to show his disenchantment with politics, and a subsequent owner gave it his own pen-name 'Master of the Fishing Nets' as a happy allusion to the original name.

The scholars had pavilions to watch moonlight on water, others to view the flowering of the plum and apricot trees. Covered verandahs let them listen to the sound of wind in the trees, or of rain on broad leaves. Open spaces were paved with wonderful patterns of pebbles and tiles; walls were white to better show plant silhouettes and shadows, and perforated by elaborately latticed windows to give teasing views of the spaces beyond.

Orchids (especially the wonderful green *Cymbidium sinense*), camellias, chrysanthemums and more were planted in handsome containers. Bonsai (*p'en ching*) trees, sometimes singly or sometimes in whole groves, were grown on broad earthenware trays, the most desirable made from the violet clays of I-hsing, near Shanghai. These were fired to a deep maroon, and often had a subtle lustre.

The plants of the open gardens were hugely important in ways that tend to surprise Western gardeners. Gardens were planned not only for form and colour but for sound as well: the sighing of wind in bamboo groves, or

Buildings, water, sky, rocks, plants – this part of the Suzhou garden is almost a garden turned inside out, because the garden itself is the frame around a pool that reflects sky, pines and pavilions. Elsewhere, endless clever pieces of design beguile the garden visitor into exploring and admiring even the tiniest spaces.

through pine branches, the tuneful rasping of cicadas in their favourite willows, or the pattering of rain on banana leaves. There were, and still are, splendid traditional planting combinations: magnolias (especially *Magnolia denudata*) with herbaceous peonies beneath, chrysanthemums, pines and bamboo. In spite of all the tradition, Chinese gardeners also collected exotic plants as avidly as any other – early-18th-century paintings show them growing American cactuses, as well as Dutch tulips. Later in the century, there was a huge vogue for new roses from Paris, though Chinese gardens had plenty of wonders of their own.

The gardens were also planted for year-round pleasure. The owner could enjoy the cinnabar maples (*tan feng*) turning just that colour in autumn, and then the sight of snow on gnarled branches. After the chill delights of winter, the gardener would watch carefully every one of the unfurlings of spring. The mood of these gardens is expressed in a passage from the 18th-century Chinese novel *The Dream of the Red Chamber*, as a gardener views the garden at night.

> Moonlight, harsh and clear, floods the high pavilion. The night still young, the wicket gate is half-open. A lantern moving among trees announces the guest's arrival; smoke rises from the bamboos in answer to my call for tea. The dog barks now and then at the falling of autumn stars; gusts of wind

Left: Paved areas are treated as an integral part of the design; simple and natural materials, here pebbles carefully sorted by colour, are combined into satisfying patterns that underpin the garden structure at all times of year.

Right: The garden is planted for all aspects of a plant's possibilities – the noise of wind through its branches, or of rain on its leaves. Here, bamboo is admired for the rippling shadows it casts on a whitewashed wall.

disperse the sad sounds of a distant flute. Rapt in talk, we sit till the dawn slowly comes up, as brightly coloured clouds and cool dew overspread the green moss.

BUILDING IT

Walls here are important, being the foil to the rest of the garden and the screen against which plant shadows are cast by sun- or lantern light. They need to be 2.5m/8ft tall, and white or, better, white toned down with a dash of umber. A structure of rendered concrete block is sufficient. The walls should be coped in some manner; grand Chinese gardens like these had walls capped with glazed tiles (often green), though humbler ones were capped with thatch. Wooden shingles were sometimes used, and can look perfect. The capping needs to project from the wall by 6cm/2½in or so to take rainwater well away from the pristine wall surface. In China, garden walls were often made merely of compacted mud and straw, and so they had to be kept dry. The walls rendered with white plaster were sometimes also waxed, not only to waterproof them but to give a handsome translucent sheen to the surface.

The plan proposes a circular 'moon gate' to allow a partial view of the planting at the far end of the garden. In the scholars' gardens, these expensive features were given even more emphasis by carved stone margins that followed the curve. In lieu of stonework, you could incise the render with grooves at 4cm/1½in and 2cm/¾in along the gate's edge, and paint the edge and reveal a dark grey. If you want a window behind the *Magnolia denudata* branches, showing the plum branches beyond, choose one of the many fascinating shapes used in China – vases, pumpkins, ovals, triangles, oblongs and more. These

In Chinese gardens, doors and windows have many elegant shapes; here a circular opening gives a tantalizing view of another part of the garden, but such internal windows can be oval, vase-, even gourd-shaped.

viewing windows, designed to give enticing glimpses of gardens beyond the present one, and encouraging exploration and a sense of mystery, were filled with grilles of terracotta, carved alabaster, lacquered wood and so on. In simple Chinese gardens, the grilles are often of bamboo rods, sometimes criss-crossed, set in the render, then painted scarlet or Indian red.

Gateways and walls are easily built. Picturesque rocks, so beloved of Chinese gardeners, are made by nature. Even in China, they were hard to come by, and it was not unknown for 16th-century warrior-gardeners to raid gardens that had good ones. In Beijing, the emperors assembled collections of rocks, often of limestone and collected from river beds, that had been eroded into the most fantastic forms. Lesser gardeners made do with lesser stonework. Some even made do, as did many in Suzhou, with small rocks carefully mortared together into the required fantasy. Before you raid your local environment, should you live near a source of good stone, see if you can build something convincing from garden fragments. If you are far from any source, ignore the rockwork and double up the planting, with a low-growing *Acer japonicum* filling the role of the tall stone in the plan.

The pool is easily made using butyl sheeting. Ramp the sides as steeply as possible so that the water deepens quickly. Though many pools in Suzhou are now still and turbid, when the gardens were in their prime the city's water system flowed through them, keeping the water clear. If you want to arrange a waterfall, the best point of entry would be from beneath the pavilion. Even with movement, the water will breed mosquitoes, so you will need goldfish as well as bottom-feeding carp. The pool margins are disguised by rockwork or plants.

If possible, the viewing pavilion should overhang the pool edge, and its floor be raised about 75cm/30in or more above the water level. This should enable the viewer to see a reflection of the moon gate in the pool.

Paths in Chinese gardens are often miracles of decorative invention, their makers using the simplest materials. Pebbles in their natural colours and tiles set on edge are combined to make fishscale patterns (very appropriate to this garden), flowers and many other designs. Set in mortar, they make extremely hard-wearing surfaces, which are decorative without competing with the plants. These designs are, though, a labour of love to create. A mix of pea gravel and sand rolled into a hard and neutrally coloured surface will make a good substitute.

PLANTING AND MAINTAINING IT

Most of the plants in the plan will grow happily in a wide range of climates and soils. However, the scholars liked the sound of rain falling on banana leaves; in southern China, bananas grow easily but gardeners in colder climate zones will have difficulty with them. Cooler gardens can sometimes support species like the almost-hardy *Musa basjoo* and *M. velutina*. Otherwise, try canna lilies, or some of the larger-leaved gingers like *Hedychium gardnerianum*, whose flowers have a wonderful perfume.

The plan doesn't specify varieties of maple. The naming of them is confused, and varies from country to country, even from propagator to propagator, particularly with *Acer japonicum* (a Chinese species in spite of its name). It is perhaps best to use the closely related *Acer palmatum*, which has some fine forms, and I suggest using two or three different ones. Look for 'Heptalobum Rubrum' or 'Takinogawa'. If possible, each specimen in the plan should be a taller-growing variety, which can have its lower trunk cleared of branches to give a picturesque effect. Those with very spiky and dissected leaves tend to be slow growing and tightly branched.

Nor does the plan specify varieties of herbaceous and moutan peony. Both these are also confusingly named groups, and some varieties named after European actresses or aristocrats are in fact ancient Chinese garden plants. Others, given fake Chinese names, can be of modern Western origin. I suggest choosing varieties that you like, and planting them in groups of three.

All the plants on the left-hand side of the plan are Chinese. Some, like the viburnum and the camellia, were hugely admired by Chinese gardeners. Elsewhere, magnolias are planted with peonies beneath – one of the classic garden combinations in China.

Once planted, the garden won't require much maintenance for several seasons. The bamboo clumps will thicken up and begin to expand. The reason why they look so good in Chinese gardens is that the clumps are continuously thinned out, the three-season-old canes being removed. This is done to let in the light, so that the beauty of the stems and foliage is fully revealed. In the tall species listed in the plan, this can easily be achieved with secateurs or loppers.

The orchids must be the Chinese varieties of cymbidium, all heavily perfumed, and with flowers in bronzes, greens, greenish whites. Chinese cymbidium pots are tall and narrow, often glazed and painted, and with ventilation as well as drainage holes. Bring the plants indoors in winter, and they should flower well. The cymbidium is a symbol of virtuosity and friendship. Confucius, around 500 BC, wrote comfortingly:

A solitary Orchid, stands, adorning the side
of a mountain, perfuming the air even in the
absence of appreciation; a true scholar,
learned in morality and philosophy, is always
a gentleman, even in the absence of wealth.

Bear in mind that the Chinese garden focusses an intense awareness of the seasons and the changes wrought on the plants, which gives it a symbolic significance that transcends its physical boundaries. Rocks (however built), water, plants will make it a miniature world.

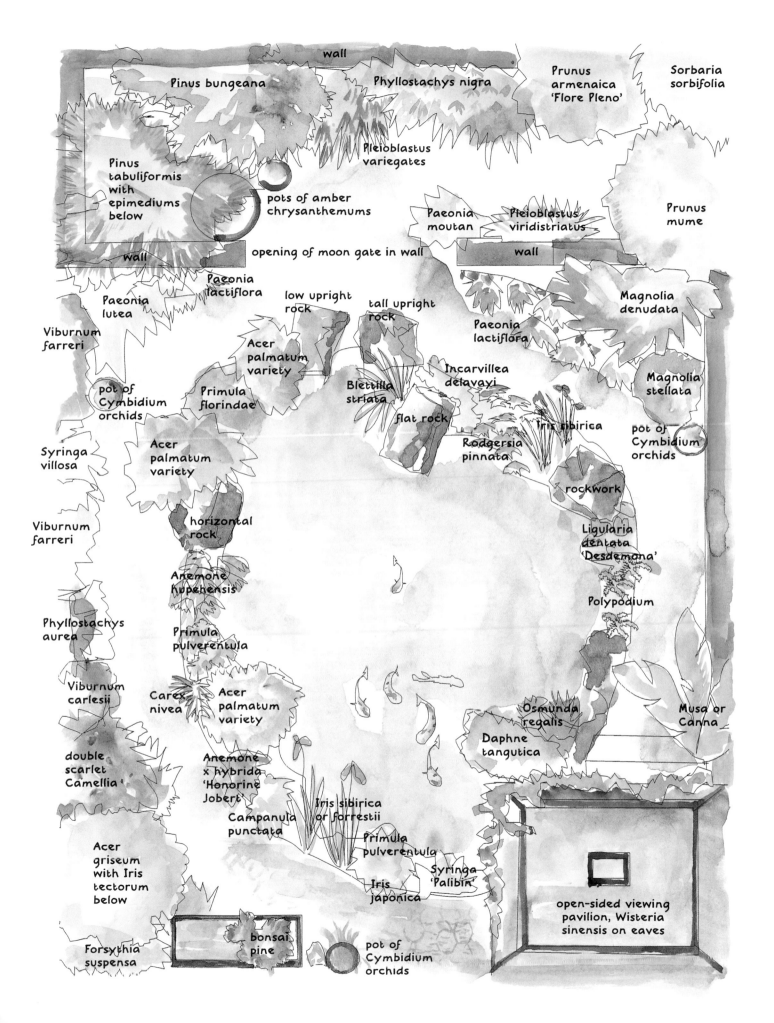

wall

Pinus bungeana

Phyllostachys nigra

Prunus armenaica 'Flore Pleno'

Sorbaria sorbifolia

Pleioblastus variegates

Pinus tabuliformis with epimediums below

pots of amber chrysanthemums

Paeonia moutan

Pleioblastus viridistriatus

Prunus mume

wall

wall

opening of moon gate in wall

Paeonia lactiflora

Magnolia denudata

Paeonia lutea

low upright rock

tall upright rock

Paeonia lactiflora

Viburnum farreri

Acer palmatum variety

Incarvillea delavayi

Magnolia stellata

pot of Cymbidium orchids

Primula florindae

Blettilla striata

flat rock

Iris sibirica

pot of Cymbidium orchids

Acer palmatum variety

Rodgersia pinnata

Syringa villosa

rockwork

Viburnum farreri

horizontal rock

Ligularia dentata 'Desdemona'

Polypodium

Anemone hupehensis

Phyllostachys aurea

Primula pulverentula

Viburnum carlesii

Carex nivea

Acer palmatum variety

Osmunda regalis

Musa or Canna

Daphne tangutica

double scarlet Camellia

Anemone x hybrida 'Honorine Jobert'

Acer griseum with Iris tectorum below

Campanula punctata

Iris sibirica or forrestii

Primula pulverentula

Syringa 'Palibin'

Iris japonica

Forsythia suspensa

bonsai pine

pot of Cymbidium orchids

open-sided viewing pavilion, Wisteria sinensis on eaves

SHOPPING LIST

HERBACEOUS PLANTING

3 *Anemone x hybrida* 'Honorine Jobert'
3 *Anemone hupehensis*
6 *Bletilla striata*
6 *Campanula punctata*
3 *Carex nivea*
9 *Chrysanthemum*, bronze, yellow, white
3 *Cymbidium sinense* or *C. ensifolium*
15 *Epimedium*
6 *Incarvillea delavayi*
6 *Iris japonica*
3 *Iris sibirica* or *I. forrestii*
12 *Iris tectorum*
3 *Ligularia dentata* 'Desdemona'
1 *Musa* or *Canna*
3 *Osmunda regalis*
9 *Paeonia lactiflora* varieties in groups of 3
3 *Phyllostachys aurea*
2 *Phyllostachys nigra*
6 *Pleioblastus variegatus*
3 *Pleioblastus viridistriatus*
3 *Polypodium*
6 *Primula florindae*
12 *Primula pulverentula*
3 *Rodgersia pinnata*

SHRUBS

1 *Camellia*, a double scarlet
3 *Daphne tangutica*
1 *Forsythia suspensa*
1 *Paeonia delavayi* var. *lutea*
3 *Paeonia moutan*
1 *Sorbaria sorbifolia*
3 *Syringa meyeri* 'Palibin'
1 *Syringa villosa*
1 *Viburnum carlesii*
2 *Viburnum farreri*
1 *Wisteria sinensis*

TREES

1 *Acer griseum*
3 *Acer palmatum* varieties
1 bonsai pine
1 *Magnolia denudata*
2 *Magnolia stellata*
1 *Pinus bungeana*
1 *Pinus tabuliformis*
1 *Prunus armeniaca* 'Flore Pleno'
1 *Prunus mume*

Opposite above: *Cymbidium sinense*
Opposite below: *Camellia 'Arbutus Gem'*
Left: *Phyllostachys aurea*
Above: *Paeonia lutea*
Below left: *Acer palmatum 'Inazuma'*
Below right: *Chrysanthemum 'George Griffith'*

THE MEDITATION GARDEN

KOBORI ENSHU AND THE NANZENJI GARDEN

GARDENS CAN MAKE WONDERFUL PLACES for meditation, whether they are little more than a few flowers in a tub, or embrace a whole landscape. Some gardens in Japan have been designed especially for contemplation. This is one of the most beautiful, and is at Nanzenji temple (Southern Mountain Temple), seat of the Rinzai sect of Zen Buddhism. The temple complex contains several gardens designed by Kobori Enshu (1579–1649), the leading architect and designer, and exponent of the tea ceremony (*cha-no-yu*). None of the others is so spare and stripped down: this one is a composition of raked gravel, wonderfully placed rocks, blank walls and a lightly planted landscape. The others, seen through open screens at the ends of corridors or long chambers, seem almost like pieces of scrubland, or are more conventional gardens with pools, bridges, rockwork and luxuriant plants. This garden, so often photographed, and so beautiful, is the most serene of them all.

However, in all these gardens, nothing is quite what it seems. Even in the apparently natural scrub gardens, plants are carefully controlled in the most detailed way. In this gravel garden, the smaller rhododendrons and azaleas are clipped into low cushions of greenery, their flowering all but suppressed. The pines are treated as if they were large bonsai, the branches tied and bent into position, the bunches of needles carefully thinned. The plums are given only slightly more latitude. Although this garden at Nanzenji is not as austere as the pure and completely plantless gravel garden of Ryoan-ji in Kyoto, here the plants become emblems of themselves, sculptures that change with the seasons, rather than plants growing pretty much as they please, as in Western gardens like Sissinghurst or Hummelo.

The extreme sophistication of these Zen gardens is matched by the high quality of materials used in the garden: there are pavilions of rare woods, lacquered screens, paintings, wonderful stonework. As with monasteries and abbeys in the West, Japanese temples became, and some remain, hugely wealthy. At Nanzenji, the wealth predated the temple, for it was originally an imperial palace. In 1290, the first Zen monk was given a pavilion, and gradually a monastery grew at the expense of secular power. Little remains from that time, for the monastery has been destroyed and rebuilt several times through its long history.

At Nanzenji, the temple gardens are designed to provide serene settings as an aid to meditation and self-awareness. Though the effect is soothing and restful, in gardening terms spaces like these are the result of extreme control of the plants. None are allowed free rein. These are symbolic landscapes, often hard to copy within other cultures; the plan here suggests some alternative approaches.

The garden is, in essence, a complete landscape, as are many Japanese gardens – and one derived from the 'tray gardens' popular in China and Japan, where miniature landscapes are created from sand, stones and bonsai on earthenware trays the size of a large plate. Here, the gravel forms an unchanging sea, the back wall a neutral sky.

NOTES ON THE PLAN

Gardens like this one, products as they are of a very particular mind-set – intense and very inward – are hard to transplant. The stone element is especially difficult; the stones were deliberately chosen and disposed as part of a contemplative process that can still be felt. The plan makes no attempt to copy the disposition of stones here – the Tiger and her Cubs – but merely places them in a way that suits the space available. If you can find good stones, do the same thing. It is the overall feel of contemplation that is important, not the copying of Nanzenji; after all, an atmosphere that is conducive to meditation can be created from many sources.

Right: In another of the gardens at Nanzenji, a symbolic arrangement of rocks and shrubs is caught in a frame from the viewing pavilion. The shrubs have been artfully pruned so that the drumstick shapes and cascade of red maple seem to tower over the rocky landscape below. The eaves of the building block out the sky, making the foliage glow.

Far right: A whole forest landscape writ small is kept in check by minutely careful pruning; this forest fragment terminates the view down a long hallway, and the magic is increased by the reflections in the tray of water.

BUILDING IT

The site is gently landscaped. Obviously, the 'sea' of gravel must be flat, but build up the planting area very gently, as if it were an emerging landmass. Ideally, the 'sea' needs to be 30cm/12in lower than the access surface to the meditation pavilion, here suggested as decking. If you need to excavate to achieve this, use the spoil to make the landscape, piling it towards the backdrop wall. The pavilion is important, and needs to give a feeling, at least inside, of security and serenity. The eaves of the roof should sweep low, so that the view of sky and distracting surroundings (especially of neighbouring houses) is cut out. Screening off the real sky makes the garden seem to glow with light, and the blank back wall stand in for the empyrean. The inside of viewing pavilions is often painted a deep earth red, a colour that makes the green of the plants even more intense. As the meditator can't see the outside of the pavilion, it need not look especially Japanese, though it would be appropriate to the overall feel of the garden if it did. Check whether local planning regulations have any impact on its construction.

The decking extends beyond the pavilion, in case you should feel like doing a walking meditation. A good-looking wooden surface makes a better walkway, and is much cheaper than high-quality stone.

The 'sky' wall needs to be around 2m/6½ft high, coped with tiles or shingles. Rendered concrete block is an ideal material. Some of the Nanzenji gardens are enclosed with wooden palisades – baulks of timber with pointed tops, some left natural, others whitened.

The sand or gravel for the 'sea' needs to be as neutral a colour as possible. Gravel should be 'pea' gravel, or even finer graded. To rake into satisfactory patterns it must be at least 8cm/3in deep, set over a base of landscape netting. Some gravel gardens blend in gravel a tone or two paler along the shoreline.

The stones are the most difficult element to find. They need to be, or to look as if they are, bedded deeply into the soil, with perhaps one surface appearing through the vegetation so that they resemble smooth glaciated rocks that have been in place for millennia. If good stones are not to be had, substitute with plants (more of the small-leaved rhododendrons, or something like *Cotoneaster horizontalis*) clipped into rock-like shapes.

PLANTING AND MAINTAINING IT

Unlike most gardens, this one needs poor soil; indeed the whole thing could easily be built on a solid foundation, a concreted yard say, though plants would need careful watering in summer. The base planting – the low-growing greenery beneath the rhododendrons and pines – makes use of typical rock garden flora. The plan suggests an overall planting of the tiny creeping bronze-green *Acaena microphylla*. This grows without much attention, and won't mind being trodden on when the rhododendrons and azaleas need clipping and the pines need training. However, depending on what does well in your region, others worth having might include *Arenaria balearica*, *Silene acaulis*, *Salix reticulata* and *Trachelium asperuloides*. Some European Zen gardens make use of the tiny weed

Sagina procumbens. If you garden somewhere with an oceanic climate, various mosses will look most authentically Japanese.

Of the other plants, the rhododendrons and azaleas need clipping once after the flowering season is over. Treat the growing pines as bonsai: bend stems into position and tie in place, or bind them to wires and bend into shape. Prune out so that the form of each plant remains open, and makes a handsome pattern against the plain wall behind.

The plan takes a liberty with the Nanzenji planting and adds the wonderful and naturally picturesque *Mahonia japonica*. This needs only occasional work, if it threatens to grow too large. Cut out whole stems as required. Use the species, not any of the named hybrids: the crosses often seem to have no smell but the species, flowering in early spring, has a wonderful perfume. It also has a much better growth form.

The plan adds a simple circular tank to the decking, in which to grow a lotus plant (*Nelumbo nucifera*) if your garden has warm summers, or one of the blue waterlilies if it is rather cooler. *Nymphaea capensis* is a stunning plant that will do in a tank of this size; N. 'Blue Beauty' is easier to find. In colder gardens a clump of Japanese iris will have to suffice. *Iris ensata* 'Blue Peter' is a European name for a plant very similar to the dark indigo and broad-petalled iris often painted on 17th-century Japanese screens. Grow with its pot submerged during the growing season, but remove in autumn. Add liquid feed to the water every few weeks, and the plants will do well. Clip off dead foliage when resubmerging the plants in the following spring. There will be a mat of greenish roots emerging from the bottom of the pot. Leave well alone. When repotting cut the probably plastic pot from around them, then divide the rhizomes.

Fallen leaves and flowers will be a nuisance. Cats and weed seedlings will spoil the perfection of your gravel too. The Nanzenji garden has a large and assiduous staff; in a lesser garden, the nuisances need themselves to become material for meditation.

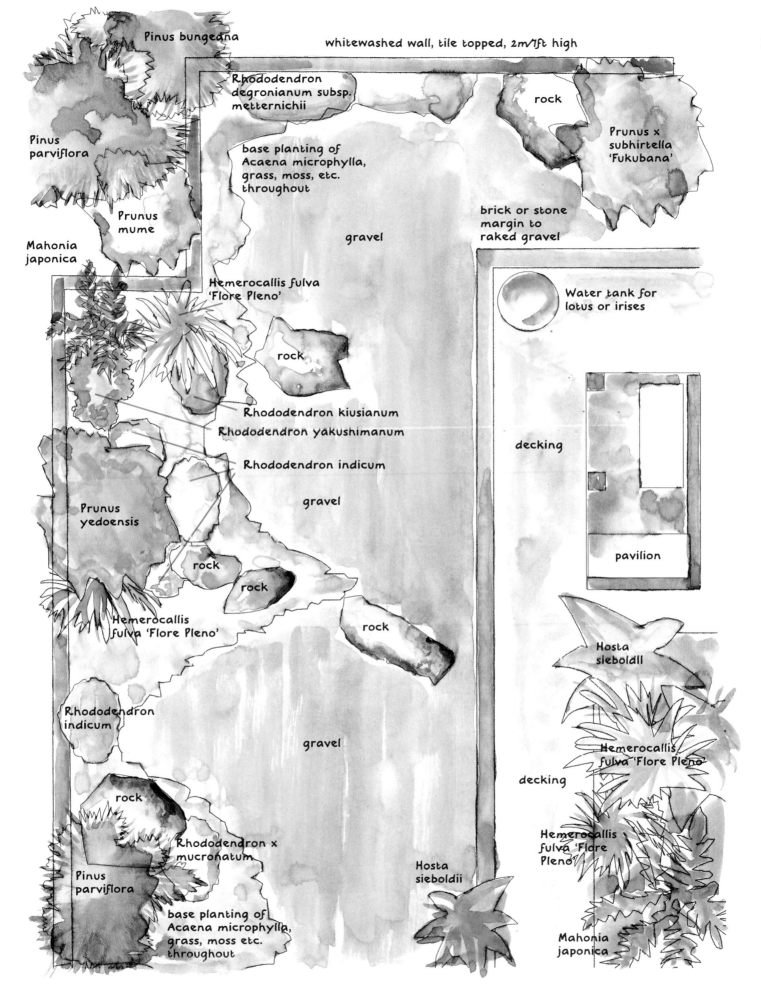

Pinus bungeana

Rhododendron
degronianum subsp.
metternichii

rock

Pinus
parviflora

Prunus x
subhirtella
'Fukubana'

base planting of
Acaena microphylla,
grass, moss, etc.
throughout

Prunus
mume

brick or stone
margin to
raked gravel

gravel

Mahonia
japonica

Hemerocallis fulva
'Flore Pleno'

Water tank for
lotus or irises

rock

Rhododendron kiusianum

Rhododendron yakushimanum

decking

Rhododendron indicum

Prunus
yedoensis

gravel

pavilion

rock

rock

rock

Hemerocallis
fulva 'Flore Pleno'

Hosta
sieboldii

Rhododendron
indicum

Hemerocallis
fulva 'Flore Pleno'

gravel

decking

Hemerocallis
fulva 'Flore
Pleno'

rock

Rhododendron x
mucronatum

Pinus
parviflora

Hosta
sieboldii

base planting of
Acaena microphylla,
grass, moss etc.
throughout

Mahonia
japonica

SHOPPING LIST

AQUATIC PLANTING
3 *Iris ensata* (syn. *I. kaempferi*), 1 blue *Nymphaea* or 1 *Nelumbo nucifera* (lotus)

HERBACEOUS PLANTING
9 *Hemerocallis fulva* 'Flore Pleno'
9 *Hosta sieboldii*
200 *Acaena microphylla*

SHRUBS
3 *Mahonia japonica*
4 *Rhododendron indicum*
1 *Rhododendron kiusianum*
1 *Rhododendron degronianum* subsp. *metternichii*
1 *Rhododendron* x *mucronatum*
1 *Rhododendron yakushimanum*

TREES
1 *Pinus bungeana*
2 *Pinus parviflora*
1 *Prunus mume*
1 *Prunus* x *subhirtella* 'Fukubana'
1 *Prunus* x *yedoensis*

Below: *Prunus* x *yedoensis*
Opposite:
Top left: *Mahonia japonica*
Top centre: *Iris kaempferi*
Top right: *Hemerocallis fulva* 'Flore Pleno'
Below left: *Rhododendron* x *mucronatum*
Below right: *Pinus bungeana*

THE MOONLIGHT GARDEN

DESIGNS FOR RAJPUT PRINCESSES
AT THE AMBER PALACE, JAIPUR

THERE ARE TWO SETS OF GARDENS in the old Rajput fortress-palace of Amber. One, exquisitely patterned with narrow marble paths, is on an artificial island built high above the water; the other is set deep within the walls of the citadel. The Rajputs were a Hindu warrior clan who furnished much of the military might of the Mughal emperors of what is now northern India. In doing so, especially in the 17th century, they accumulated huge wealth, and though they didn't follow their rulers' Islamic beliefs, they copied their sophisticated lifestyle, especially in the matter of gardens.

Rajput as well as Mughal palaces housed the harem. Wives and concubines were not allowed into the fabulous gardens during the day, and so moonlight gardens were planted for them, filled with pale-coloured flowers to reflect moon- and starlight, and often with perfume too. Even by the 17th century, when much of Amber was rebuilt, moonlight gardens were an ancient idea. The Mughal emperor Babur (1483–1530), who first defeated and then recruited the Rajputs, had one for his womenfolk, filled with narcissus and red and white oleanders. Shah Jahan (1592–1666) built one, called as they all are Mahtab Bagh, at Shahjahanabad. It was filled with fruit trees and narcissus. He also built a moonlight garden on the river bank opposite the tomb to his wife, the Taj Mahal. This forgotten space, only now being excavated, had a pool to reflect the astonishing beauty of the building. Water was supplied in the traditional manner, through spring-fed runnels of carved marble.

Rajput and Mughal gardeners were acquisitive of lovely plants. One of the most complete lists is for a late-17th-century moonlight garden in the ancient Red Fort at Delhi. The list ran from native jasmines (especially the gorgeous *Jasminum sambac*, the most strongly perfumed of the genus) to gardenias, lotuses, the American cactus *Selenicereus grandiflorus*, whose vast flowers last only for one night, the wonderful annual climber called the 'moonflower' (*Ipomoea alba*, syn. *Calonyction speciosum*), tuberose, Mexican daturas, Peruvian petunias, stephanotis and magnolias. One of the rooms overlooking the garden was adorned with the inscription 'If there be paradise on earth, it is this, it is this, it is this . . . '. The rivulet

The harsh grandeur of the Rajasthani landscape surrounds the civilized elegance of the Amber Palace's colonnades and formal gardens; the latter were once filled with lilies and stocks, stephanotis and jasmine, all best appreciated by star- and candlelight.

of water that ran through palace and garden was called the Nahir-i-Bihisht, or the Stream of Paradise.

Alas, all the gardens are now almost empty or even derelict, except for a few specimens of bougainvillea, a plant which was only introduced in the late 18th century. The mind's eye must see the spaces filled with the plants listed here, and the gardens surrounded by even more magnificence, for the now bare arcades and shadowy rooms were once encrusted with marble inlaid with precious stones, the ceilings covered in silver and gold.

NOTES ON THE PLAN

A summer's night in the garden can be very special, and if you hardly see your garden during a busy day, then one designed for night is even more to be treasured. The magnificence of the Amber Palace can't be emulated, but all its plants are easy to grow, and can give you as much pleasure as they did the Rajput court.

The plan envisages a Rajput parterre in a sunken garden centred on a shallow and simple octagonal pool. The raised side beds are to give a boundary and a planting area for shrubs with perfumed flowers. If your site doesn't lend itself easily to changes in level, then suppress the steps and treat the entire plan as flat. The parterre is treated as a bedding garden, with the plants needing to be stripped out and replanted twice a year, once at the end of the spring flowering of bulbs, and once as winter comes on.

The terrace areas at each end of the plan offer places from which to view the garden beneath the stars, and to savour the perfumes. One has a small square pool for waterlilies or, if your garden is warm enough, lotuses. The other has a large raised platform to stand in as a Mughal throne, and is intended to be adorned with carpets and some big cushions.

BUILDING IT

In both garden areas of the Amber Palace, whether the huge moated parterres or the guarded gardens of the citadel, most of the garden details, paths, wall coverings and pools are or were made of marble. Here,

concrete is substituted; however, sensitively done, with smooth surfaces in natural colours, it can still look good. Alternatively, for all hard surfaces use bricks in a good earthen red, set on edge.

The paths, narrow enough for a single moonlight watcher to move through the flower beds, need to be trim-edged, with the intersections handled cleanly. In Mughal and Rajput gardens, the intersections would have been emphasized in some way, perhaps with star-shaped insets of marble or brilliantly coloured tiles.

Mughal designers and gardeners had a passion for water. A vital feature in gardens, it flowed along rills and channels, was sprayed through fountains, and was allowed to cascade down splendidly carved water-chutes, surround thrones and pavilions, or rest briefly in marble tanks. Here, a vertical-sided pool would be fine, though the plan suggests a design based on the small pool from the moonlight garden opposite the Taj Mahal. In that, the interior was stepped, perhaps to give a heightened colour to the water with each increase in depth. The steps are most easily managed inside a waterproofed excavation, using brick or concrete blocks and finishing the surface with a skim of concrete. If possible, arrange to have a central fountain; a Mughal one would have had an elaborately turned brass spout. The pool doesn't need to be deep, being intended, when still, as a mirror; 60cm/2ft is enough. If the sides are stepped, give each step around 10cm/4in depth, with a platform of 30cm/1ft. The best

Top right: Other gardens at the Amber Palace are even more intricately formal; this one is an island, on three levels so that the patterns are more easily appreciated, with intricate balustrading surrounding viewing terraces.

Bottom right: The parterre patterns are made of filigrees of cut marble that once enclosed plantings of bulbs and perfumed flowers. The planting areas are sunk, to make watering simpler, but also to keep the level of the flowers close to the level of the paths and to form a flowering carpet.

Opposite: *Matthiola bicornis*
Top left: *Hesperis matronalis*
Top centre: *Heliotropium 'Marine'*
Top right: *Gardenia jasminoides*
Centre left: *Rhododendron luteum*
Centre right: Blue waterlily (*Nymphaea*)
Bottom left: *Lunaria rediviva*
Bottom right: *Hyacinthus 'Yellow Queen'*

A BAROQUE PARTERRE GARDEN

DANIEL MAROT AT HET LOO PALACE

T HIS RE-CREATION OF THE GARDENS designed for William of Orange, later the joint ruler, with his wife Mary, of Britain, at the woodland hunting palace of the rulers of the Netherlands has become a classic showpiece of the Dutch baroque garden style. The original designs were drawn up by Daniel Marot (1661–1752) in the early 1680s; documents describe him as a mathematician, which he may have considered himself to be, though he is best known for his designs for gardens and interior decor. Though he worked mostly for aristocratic French patrons, in Holland he adapted to Dutch sensibilities and designed a garden that, though grand and costly, was entirely scaleable – the same idiom and the same planting could be used in the backyard of a tiny house in Amsterdam or Haarlem, and looked as good as it did at palace scale. Many pretty examples can still be found. In France, the immense schemes of André le Nôtre, or even those of Marot for French patrons, worked only at the very grandest scale, and so were of no use to minor gardeners.

The charm of these Dutch baroque gardens is that they not only make a showground for interesting plants, but are attractive throughout the year. Their structure lasts almost unchanged through the seasons. They can look as entrancing under snow as they do in highest summer. They are as pleasing from a window as they are to wander through, or to view from a trellis-shaded seat. And for lovers of symmetry and order, they are perfect.

They do, though, require work. Dutch gardeners were, and often still are, exceedingly diligent. In the scheme suggested, the planting spaces need clearing and refilling twice a year. The bulbs need drying and sorting, unless you plan to repurchase every autumn. Plants need raising from seed for some of the summer planting. The box hedges need at least one pruning a year to keep them sharp. The gravel needs to be kept clear of weeds and fallen leaves. Trellis, unless you have rot-proofed it, needs maintenance and repair after its first few crisp seasons. The grass, if you leave the pair of topmost sections empty, needs constant cutting and weeding. It is a garden of artifice and effort.

NOTES ON THE PLAN

Though the garden at Het Loo has some exciting waterworks, the plan shows none. If water is important for you, then narrow canals could be cut

At Het Loo, as in other gardens of its time, a two-dimensional pattern is sovereign. Parterres were designed to be seen from above, particularly from the house, but also from the elevated walks along the margins of the garden. Only the ever-attentive gardeners set foot on the parterres themselves; owners and courtiers strolled the walks, perhaps observing the rare or beautiful plants growing in the outermost bands of each pattern.

running the length of the two central sections, and between the topiary obelisks and globes. The plan also does not commit itself as to the nature of the centrepieces for the lower pair of parterres, or the upper grass plat areas. Princely gardens used statuary, but good garden pieces now cost princely sums. It is hard to find good reproductions at all, and impossible to find anything worth using at most garden centres. Good reproduction urns, in both concrete (even if called reconstituted stone) or fibreglass, are much easier to find. Better still, the larger garden centres sell, or can order, quite good pieces of topiary, often grown in traditional shapes that fit perfectly into parterre gardens. Alternatively, you could centre the parterre on a large earthenware pot, filled with a dramatic plant – something too large or too floppy to go in the narrow planting beds edging the parterres: for example, an oleander, or a brugmansia or even a luxuriant planting of dusky red nicotianas.

The corners of the garden are planted with trees to give some suggestion of the wild landscape beyond the artifice of the parterres. The woodland of the landscape at Het Loo has formal rides cut through it for hunting.

BUILDING IT

In a garden like this, modern plastics are a huge help. The woven nylon sheeting called 'landscape netting' is especially good. It makes a perfect base for paths, for the gravel infill of the box curlicues, as a weed suppressant, wormcast deterrent and much more. Most sorts even have a grid of coloured strands to help with the placing of the design.

Paths first: brick, as usual, can look enchanting, ideally antique handmade bricks, a bit worn and rounded, placed on edge in a weave or herringbone

At Het Loo, arbours of hornbeam, tied into vast, airy frameworks, offer shady places from which to view the resplendent patterned garden, in which flowers play a relatively minor role.

Above: Seating and some of the architectural detailing at Het Loo was, and is, made of trelliswork of great elaboration. This close-up of a grand seat-back shows elegant design and craftsmanship.

Left: The high walks of a baroque garden, sometimes called 'mounts', offered not only seating from which to view the parterres, but also sites for elaborate cascades and tiers of fountains. The mounts and the parterres themselves were given some vertical emphasis by the use of clipped obelisks of yew or cypress; the ones shown here are still young.

pattern. They can be easily laid on netting with a finger's width left between them. Brush a dry fifty-fifty mix of sand and cement between the bricks, firm down, then sprinkle with water. Alternatively you can use all sand between the bricks; though this is less stable, and provides a fine germination ground for weed seedlings, the path can easily be altered or repaired. If you do not want brick, use a pea gravel and sand mix for the path. The sand stops the gravel grinding when you tread on it, and the mix soon compacts to make a good surface for walking. It is also resistant to scuffing, and the plastic sheeting remains hidden. Sand, particularly if not clean, can clog the netting and cause drainage problems, but these are easily cured by puncturing the puddle's base with a garden fork.

The planting area between the pair of outer box margins is best left completely clear of netting, which can become a nuisance if it begins to unweave. The nylon strands cut hands, and tangle trowels and handforks. If you use netting under paths, cut and pin down margins with U-shaped pins made of galvanized wire, 7cm/3in long, hammered into the soil. The whole parterre region can be netted, and cuts made in the netting wherever a young box plant is to go. Fill the remaining area with light and dark gravels. Use river gravels, which have a nicer texture than crushed stone.

The trelliswork is made almost entirely of horizontal and vertical slats. The plan suggests enclosing the whole garden in trellis. A small parterre works best in enclosed spaces, so that the observer's eye is kept on the garden's detail. If you don't care for trellis, enclose with hedging. Yew is perfect, but holly is faster and equally in period, though picking up the clippings is a chore and fallen leaves are not much fun if you like walking in your garden barefoot. The trellis should be painted a rich mid-blue.

Pots and tubs are an important element in the garden. If possible, use terracotta pots, ideally decorated with swags, masks and so on. Versailles tubs painted deep blue or green are perfect containers for orange or lemon trees. Glazed blue and white pots were popular for smaller 'greens', but good contemporary ones can still be found, or can be made.

The side benches would only have been stone slabs supported on classical brackets. Good copies are easily available. The seat at the top of the garden should be more comfortable – made of wood, and painted in the same colour as the surrounding trellis.

PLANTING AND MAINTAINING IT

The box hedging offers no difficulties. At the planting distances suggested, two or three seasons will pass before you have a joined-up hedge. In very cold regions where box won't grow, try whortleberry (blaeberry) (*Vaccinium myrtillus*) or other local species of *Vaccinium*. Otherwise, box is tough. It gets occasional aphid infestations, but is never much damaged. It does, though, make a perfect hiding place for snails. A summer shower can bring so many to the surface of the hedge that twigs bend with the weight. Remove them.

For the planted bands around the parterre/plat areas, the design suggests two schemes for spring, one to be used on one pair of matching beds, the other on the other pair. In summer, the pots and tubs will provide enough to look at, so only one bedding scheme is given. The spring and summer schemes are marked by numbers on the plan, and are detailed on the shopping list.

The shopping list makes suggestions for what goes in the pots on the terrace area of the plan. In the 17th century, exotic plants were beginning to reach Europe from North and Central America, from the Middle East and India. Advances in glass technology provided orangeries for even quite modest gardeners to overwinter citrus plants, myrtles, persimmons or pomegranates, Carolina allspice and more. Even the classical olive, with its silvery foliage and picturesque way of growing, can look wonderful if overwintered away from the worst frosts. Smaller plants, including bulbs like sprekelia, eucomis, crinum, even the charming *Mirabilis jalapa*, are all good. Exotic architectural plants like the agave of Central America or the aloes of Africa also look handsome.

47

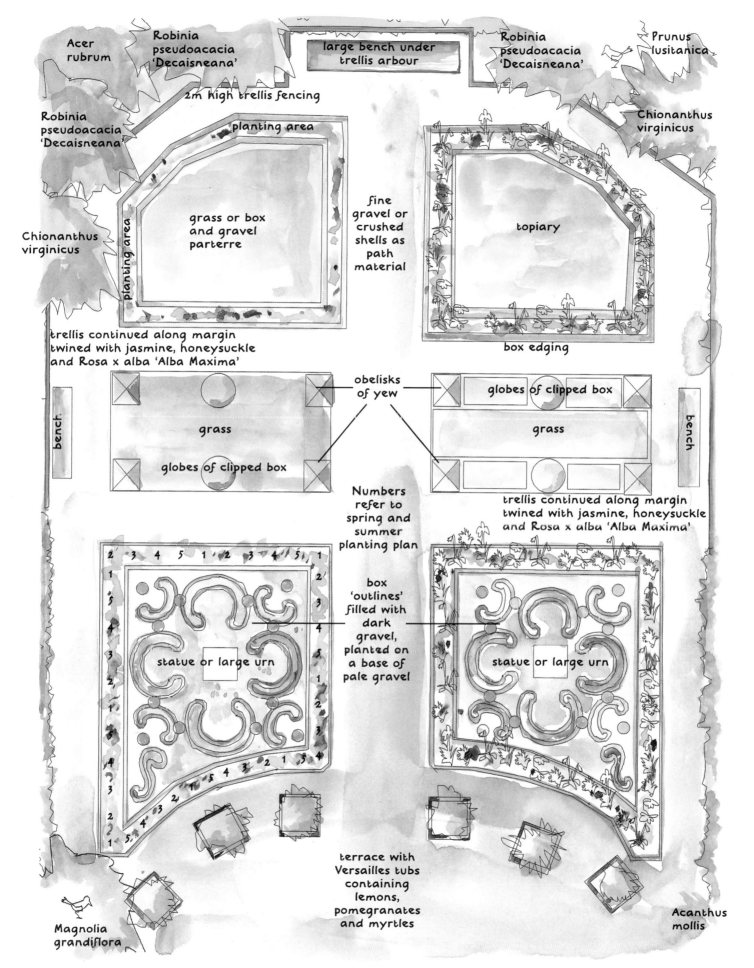

SHOPPING LIST

PARTERRE/PLAT PLANTING

SPRING SCHEME A

BULBS

30 *Fritillaria imperialis*

180 *Muscari armeniacum* 'Fantasy Creation' in 6s

180 *Anemone coronaria* De Caen Group, blue in 6s

30 *Fritillaria persica* 'Adiyaman'

90 *Tulipa* 'Rembrandt' in 3s

SPRING SCHEME B

BULBS

90 *Tulipa* 'Black Parrot' in 3s

90 *Hyacinthus orientalis* 'Carnegie' in 3s

90 *Narcissus* 'Telamonius Plenus' (syn. 'Van Sion') in 3s

90 *Anemone* x *fulgens* in 3s

90 *Narcissus jonquilla* in 3s

SUMMER SCHEME

SEED

30 *Celeosia argentea* var. *cristata* Plumosa Group

90 *Matthiola incana* (summer stocks), white, in 3s

90 *Amaranthus tricolor* in 3s

30 *Convolvulus tricolor*

BULBS

90 *Lilium martagon* var. *album* in 3s

PERMANENT PLANTING

HERBACEOUS PLANTING

3 *Acanthus mollis*

SHRUBS

2000 *Buxus sempervirens* (box)

8 *Jasminum officinale*

8 *Lonicera periclymenum* 'Belgica' (early Dutch honeysuckle)

8 *Rosa* x *alba* 'Alba Maxima'

TREES

1 *Acer rubrum*

2 *Chionanthus virginicus*

2 *Citrus limon* (lemons) or *C. auranticum* (oranges)

1 *Magnolia grandiflora*

2 *Myrtus communis*

2 *Punica granatum* (pomegranates)

1 *Prunus lusitanica*

3 *Robinia pseudacacia* 'Decaisneana'

6 *Taxus baccata* (yew)

Opposite left: *Tulipa* 'Kaiserskroon'
Opposite right: *Citrus limon* 'Imperial'
Left: *Jasminum officinale*
Above: *Narcissus jonquilla*
Right: *Convolvulus tricolor*
Below left: *Fritillaria officinalis*
Below right: *Myrtus communis*

50

GONE WITH THE WIND

MAGNOLIAS AND AZALEAS
IN THE SOUTHERN STATES OF THE USA

THE GREAT PLANTATION ESTATES of the Old South, Louisiana and the Carolinas especially, had, and still have, some remarkable gardens. The wonderful approach avenues, lined with live oaks (*Quercus virginiana*) sumptuously draped with Spanish moss (*Tillandsia usneoides*) may indeed once have echoed the wild gallop of the menfolk dashing to battle or away from complicated relationships, but the real gardens were quieter, filled with magnolias from much further away than the local forests, and azaleas, cornus species and new camellias of both European and Japanese breeding.

Great examples like Afton Villa and Magnolia Plantation are amongst the very finest of ante-bellum gardens left in the southern states of the USA. Even though these gardens have been much replanted since the mid-18th century, American species of magnolia – especially the sumptuous *Magnolia grandiflora*, *M. fraseri* and the heavily perfumed *M. tripetala* – can all be found. However, you will also find Japanese magnolias and their hybrids, as well as the French *M. x soulangeana*, which were widely available late in the century. Early flowering, they were often teamed with huge drifts of azaleas, the varieties often originating in Europe and the Orient but soon hybridizing to produce new American sorts (the scarlet Pride of Afton, or Afton Villa Red, is one of them).

NOTES ON THE PLAN
In a small space, live oaks would soon grow impossibly large, and some of the big magnolia species, however magnificent, would soon shade all else out of the garden. Emphasis needs to shift towards some of the Japanese species, and to modern cultivars, many of which are happy, unlike some of the species, to flower as young plants.

Although the romance of these great live oaks (Quercus virginiana) *so splendidly draped with Spanish moss* (Tillandsia usneoides) *may be hard to emulate, gardeners can use the underplantings of magnolias, prunuses, camellias and azaleas to make enchanting gardens even in tiny spaces.*

Left: Here, a stone goddess stands dreaming in the shadows, forming a counterpoint to the romantic plantings around her. In a small garden, try to find something simpler to fulfil the same function. It is possible to buy excellent copies of 18th-century urns, though good contemporary sculpture can work marvellously too.

Right: A plump stone cupid like this one, backed by colourful azaleas, can focus the gardener's eye on a vista planned in a small garden, quite as well as a god or goddess can in a great one.

Magnolia stellata and its cultivars make wonderful large bushes for small gardens, and many of the other cultivars, like 'Susan', will flower in their fourth or fifth season. However, it is impossible to resist trying a few of the larger sorts, particularly the Chinese *M. campbellii* subsp. *mollicomata*, whose huge pale madder pink flowers will start appearing even on plants 5m/16½ft high. Magnolias like a certain amount of shelter, and some can be spoiled by very late frosts. This makes them especially suitable for urban, even inner-city, gardens.

The plan gives two oblique formal views, that from each corner seat centred on the decorative element – either urn or statue (there are some handsome pieces at Afton Villa). The path allows an informal ramble through, and under, the planting. The first American landscape designer and writer, Andrew Jackson Downing (1815–1852), suggested such meandering paths, following the Scots author and designer John Claudius Loudon (1783–1843), who illustrated similar ideas in his splendid *Encyclopaedia of Gardening* of 1822. The season will run from early spring to the approach of midsummer, giving you a mostly green late summer, and then a red and bronze autumn, as the azaleas and cornus trees colour and begin to close down for winter.

The intensity of the colour of the magnolia flowers is dependent on season and location. The best colours, and best perfumes, develop in the warmest gardens. Ask your supplier how specific plants will do in your area. The azaleas will ensure that you get plenty of colour while you are waiting for the magnolias.

Even the slightly tender magnolias, such as *M. grandiflora*, which needs to be grown against a wall in cold gardens, have a much wider climatic range than the Spanish moss that gives many southern gardens such character. The plan calls for substantial numbers of ground-growing ferns to make up for the loss where it won't grow. The fern suggested is the large and lovely *Polystichum setiferum*, with dense brown scales along the main leaf rib. It keeps its foliage through the winter and so gives form and atmosphere to the underplanting all year. It doesn't run or spore itself about with much enthusiasm. If you need more, half-fill half a dozen or so transparent plastic tubs left over from supermarket produce with peat- or coconut-based compost, and in early autumn put a few leaflets on the soil surface, once you've checked that they have brownish sporangiophores on their undersurface. Tape the container closed, and put somewhere shady and cool outdoors. Check occasionally that the compost is still moist. Within a season and a half you should have plenty of young plants. Harden the separated youngsters off as carefully as you would a valuable seedling.

If you can't find polystichums, *Dryopteris* species make an acceptable, though deciduous, substitute. If your garden is damp, you can also use the shuttlecock

fern (*Matteuccia struthiopteris*), which increases rapidly, has edible young fronds and is getting rare in the American wild. It is, alas, deciduous.

BUILDING IT

The path that runs around the lawn could perhaps in a modern space be made of bark chippings, though a rolled sand/gravel mix would be correct for the period. It would also be possible to leave it out altogether and just have grass. The garden could then be described as a 'wilderness', and would be as pretty, if less convenient. One sentimental writer of the period, though, advocated well-drained paths for the use of ladies, all of whom, even Scarlet O'Hara, were seen as weak and fragile beings, forever wearing satin slippers on the tiniest of feet and constantly at risk of illness from the merest touch of damp or cold.

The seats need to be generous in scale; magnolias are so wonderful in flower that they should be looked at long and comfortably. Cast iron was becoming a popular material at the time, and many handsome designs were produced. All surviving examples are now expensive, but cast aluminium reproductions are available. Few are especially comfortable. The best have cast metal ends supporting wooden planking for seat and back. They are comfortable, warm to sit on and dry quickly after rain. They look best, as they were originally, painted all over in one colour, often dark green, or sometimes wood-grained, or even finished in scarlet and gilding.

Both Magnolia Plantation and Afton Villa have some splendid decoration. The first has a wildly elegant bridge, the second much excellent statuary. In a small space, a generously scaled urn on a plinth is a good substitute. Best is an urn with the classical tazza shape, broad and shallow with handsome handles. These dry out quickly, but hold plants well. Nineteenth-century gardeners liked to have a cordyline or yucca as a central feature, encircled by abundant flowers. Here, the plan suggests scarlet petunias, plants forgiving of some drought. If the urn and base are of stone or concrete, give them a good foundation of rubble and concrete on which to stand. However firm the garden soil may seem, the constant weight will gradually compact it, and the urn may develop a list.

PLANTING AND MAINTAINING IT

Ideally, magnolias and other trees are planted a season before the underplanting goes in. This allows the ground to be weeded, and new plantings to be watered copiously. Magnolias have fleshy and rather brittle roots; untangle them as carefully as possible from the original rootball and spread out before planting. The base of the hole where they are to go can be convex, like the base of a wine bottle, to allow the roots to be spread evenly and not to be broken when soil goes in on top of them. Azaleas have a very tight and tangled rootball. Leave well alone. Plant and then keep a frequent check on the surrounding soil for the next year, making sure it doesn't dry out.

Later, put in the bulbs and small herbaceous plants. The first autumn after tree-planting would be ideal. The plan suggests the elegant white tulip 'White Triumphator', which naturalizes well. A white parrot tulip would also be fun. If you want more colour around the white azaleas, try the vigorous mid-yellow 'Mrs John T. Scheepers', each petal with a wire-thin margin of scarlet. She, too, naturalizes well. She is named after the wife of an owner of the famous American bulb nursery. If you want a red tulip for the urn, to give colour before the petunias, use the marvellous 19th-century 'Couleur Cardinal', a deep cherry red with a waxy blue wash over each petal. It's stunning, but needs lifting. If you don't like petunias, try pelargoniums. A variety popular in mid-19th-century America was called 'General Grant'.

The heucheras need to be bought in, but it is worth trying *Tolmiea menziesii* from seed. The flowers have an inflated green sepal tube, with thread-like dark brownish purple petals issuing from it. The point of growing from seed is that some individuals have a really splendid perfume. Others don't. If you have lots of seedlings you can be sure that some will. If you buy divisions from a nursery, you might miss out.

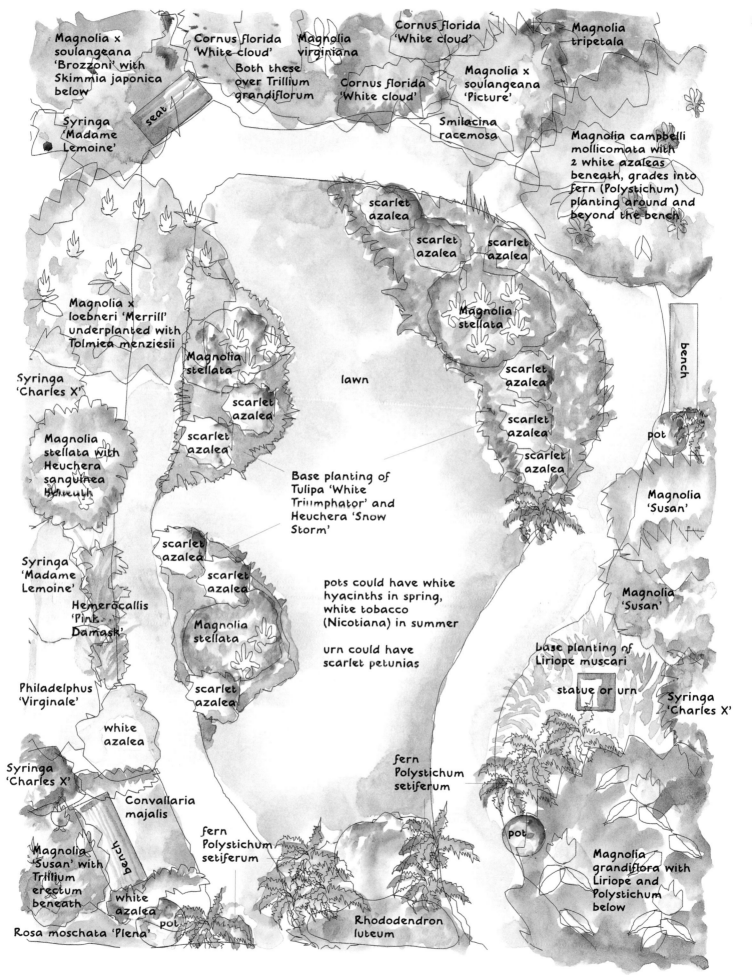

Magnolia x soulangeana 'Brozzoni' with Skimmia japonica below

Cornus florida 'White cloud'

Magnolia virginiana

Both these over Trillium grandiflorum

Cornus florida 'White cloud'

Magnolia tripetala

Cornus florida 'White cloud'

Magnolia x soulangeana 'Picture'

Smilacina racemosa

Syringa 'Madame Lemoine'

seat

Magnolia campbelli mollicomata with 2 white azaleas beneath, grades into fern (Polystichum) planting around and beyond the bench

scarlet azalea

scarlet azalea

scarlet azalea

Magnolia x loebneri 'Merrill' underplanted with Tolmiea menziesii

Magnolia stellata

Magnolia stellata

bench

Syringa 'Charles X'

scarlet azalea

lawn

scarlet azalea

scarlet azalea

scarlet azalea

scarlet azalea

pot

scarlet azalea

Magnolia stellata with Heuchera sanguinea beneath

Base planting of Tulipa 'White Triumphator' and Heuchera 'Snow Storm'

Magnolia 'Susan'

Syringa 'Madame Lemoine'

scarlet azalea

scarlet azalea

Hemerocallis 'Pink Damask'

Magnolia stellata

pots could have white hyacinths in spring, white tobacco (Nicotiana) in summer

urn could have scarlet petunias

Magnolia 'Susan'

base planting of Liriope muscari

Philadelphus 'Virginale'

scarlet azalea

statue or urn

Syringa 'Charles X'

white azalea

fern Polystichum setiferum

Syringa 'Charles X'

Convallaria majalis

bench

fern Polystichum setiferum

pot

Magnolia 'Susan' with Trillium erectum beneath

white azalea

pot

Magnolia grandiflora with Liriope and Polystichum below

Rosa moschata 'Plena'

Rhododendron luteum

SHOPPING LIST

BULBS

50 *Trillium erectum*

50 *Trillium grandiflorum*

200 *Tulipa* 'White Triumphator'

HERBACEOUS PLANTING

6 *Hemerocallis* 'Pink Damask'

50 *Heuchera sanguinea*

100 *Heuchera sanguinea* 'Snow Storm'

50 *Liriope muscari*

20 *Polystichum setiferum*

9 *Smilacina racemosa*

30 *Tolmiea menziesii*

SHRUBS

11 azalea, scarlet variety

3 azalea, white variety

1 *Philadelphus* 'Virginale'

3 *Rhododendron luteum*

1 *Rosa moschata* 'Plena'

9 *Skimmia japonica*

TREES

3 *Cornus florida* 'White Cloud'

1 *Magnolia campbelli* subsp. *mollicomata*

1 *Magnolia grandiflora*

4 *Magnolia stellata*

1 *Magnolia tripetala*

1 *Magnolia virginiana*

1 *Magnolia x loebneri* 'Merrill'

1 *Magnolia x soulangeana* 'Brozzoni'

1 *Magnolia x soulangeana* 'Picture'

3 *Magnolia x* 'Susan'

3 *Syringa vulgaris* 'Charles X'

2 *Syringa vulgaris* 'Madame Lemoine'

Near right: *Magnolia campbelli* subsp. *mollicomata*
Opposite top left: *Magnolia grandiflora*
Opposite top right: *Magnolia stellata*
Opposite centre left: *Smilacina racemosa*
Opposite centre: *Skimmia japonica*
Opposite centre right: *Trillium erectum*
Opposite bottom left: *Polystichum setiferum*
Opposite bottom right: *Liriope muscari*

A COPSE GARDEN

WILLIAM ROBINSON AT GRAVETYE MANOR

WILLIAM ROBINSON (1838–1935) was one of the most influential late-19th-century garden theorists. Starting humbly as an under-gardener on an Irish estate owned by a man he disliked, he early realized he was capable of rather higher things. As a gardener, and a considerable polemicist, he hated the vogue then current in even the grandest gardens for 'bedding plants'. He hated the artificiality of it all, the reduction of plants to the means merely of providing sheets of raucous colour. He'd found a topic upon which to attack conventional gardening and gardeners. All he needed was a platform.

At the age of twenty-three, he moved to London, and worked for the then great nursery of Veitch. Soon finding that he could turn a perfect sentence, and annoy large numbers of people, he became first a journalist, then a publishing entrepreneur. He first founded a weekly paper called *The Garden*, then, in 1879, another merely called *Gardening*. This was a huge and instant success. He assembled like-minded writers around him, notably the young Gertrude Jekyll. The magazine's continuing sales eventually enabled him to buy the house and estate of Gravetye, and a site to put his theories into practice.

Totally rejecting the horrors of annual or half-hardy bedding, he believed that gardening's aim was to produce plantings in which plants looked as natural as they did in the wild, even though they were growing in southern Britain rather than the Caucasus or the Appalachians. His wonderful, infuriating book *The Wild Garden* went through dozens of editions, the last of which appeared in 1956.

Much of the Gravetye estate had been managed as coppiced woodland, and this gave him a marvellous opportunity to experiment by planting drifts of scillas, cyclamens and narcissus between the coppiced hazels and chestnuts. On the woodland margins, or along the rides cut through it, he liked big plantings of Japanese anemones, lilies, acanthus, even pampas grass, handsome shrubs like *Fothergilla*, *Stewartia*, *Nyssa* and more. Nearer the house, though he did have flower beds and sundials, he encouraged valerian to seed into paving and staircases, and swathed the walls of the ancient house with handsome vines like the grey-leaved dusty miller (*Vitis vinifera* 'Incana'), and relatives like *Parthenocissus quinquefolia*.

William Robinson liked wild species to invade the terraces, and even the fabric, of his Elizabethan house, Gravetye Manor. Here, generous quantities of red valerian (Centranthus ruber) remain, in happy collaboration with irises, lavenders, sages and even some ericas.

NOTES ON THE PLAN

The plan is for a copse garden, the coppice being of hazels, though chestnut or even willow would give the same overall effect – a whole woodland in a little space. The tall bunches of leafy poles cast a light and dappled shade, making the ground below a perfect place to grow as much of the enchanting woodland flora as you can. The planting in the plan is really only an introduction to the masses of fine things that can be grown, and which can be of interest throughout the year, but which give their most plenteous show in spring and early summer. While a summer woodland may be low on flowers, there is nothing nicer than a seat in its luminous green shade, and the birds and insects that the shade attracts.

BUILDING IT

There is little building here at all. A small central pool, which can easily be made with butyl sheeting or by using a commercial fibreglass liner, provides the almond scent of *Aponogeton*, and should soon attract frogs, toads, newts and the occasional dragonfly. The plan shows a plinth at one side; this is meant to be a base for something decorative, whether pot, urn or the sort of bronze heron popular in the 19th century. The paths can be of mown grass, or chipped bark. The terrace near the house, where the plan suggests flowers that Robinson had near his own home, could be stone or brick paviours; Robinson's terrace was made of Ham flagstones.

The plan suggests two benches on which to enjoy the dappled shade of summer, or sort the nuts of

Far left: Here, by the house, magnolias shade a wooden seat, while beyond, sages, artemisias, helichrysums and phlomis spill over on to the path, softening the formality of the flagstones.

Left: The formal areas of the garden rapidly give way to woodland and wild areas. Beyond a simple bench and old wooden stocks, the clipped lawn changes to wild grasses edging the lake.

Though conifers have ousted the coppiced hazels and chestnuts of Robinson's time, this decorative meadow, flooded with scillas surrounding clumps of daffodils, shows the sort of effect he advocated in The Wild Garden. *Originally published in 1870, the book still offers ecologically minded gardeners one way of making an exciting garden using species adapted to the local environment.*

autumn. Simple wooden benches are fine. Later, when you have ample hazel branches, build rustic benches, and perhaps shelters for them, with the poles.

PLANTING AND MAINTAINING IT

Tree-planting is the first priority. If you decide to plant mostly hazels, your plants will arrive usually with a couple of stems, perhaps 1m/3½ft or so long. Plant in well-manured soil. They can sometimes take a while to get established and, because they are shallow-rooted, you need to make sure that they don't dry out in their first season. Four or five seasons later they will have grown to a couple of yards high, and in early spring will already be draped with long silvery yellow catkins, and the tiny tufts of velvety alizarin red styles that indicate a good crop of nuts. If you live near commercial hazel plantations your plants may suffer from fungal infections and insect predators, though in general hazels need no spraying.

While coppices were grown for their timber, you might want a nut crop too. For that, it is best to grow a range of varieties. It is actually hard to get hold of named ones, many nurseries merely selling seedlings from a plant they have as a named sort. However, if possible, look for: the delicious *Corylus avellana* 'Pearson's Prolific'; *C. maxima* (sometimes called 'Avelline'); the Turkish hazel, *C. colurna* (sometimes sold as the grand-sounding 'Impérial de Trébizonde' – though Trabzon now grows more tobacco than filberts); *C. m.* 'Kentish Cob' (or 'Lambert's Filbert'), in which the nut falls surrounded by its frilled green bracts, making it look enchanting on the plate at the end of dinner; and the high-yielding form often sold as 'White American'. There are also forms in which the usual brown skin of the ripe nut is a mahogany red. Don't plant the horrid and useless *C. a.* 'Contorta'.

The coppice 'stools' will need thinning in another few seasons; for a garden of the size specified here, cut down half of each stool about 30cm/1ft from ground level, and leave the other side alone. Let new stems grow from the cut side for two or three seasons, then cut the more mature side down. In a larger space, cut down the whole of each alternate 'stool'. Regrowth is fast. The poles make firewood, and can be used in basketwork, fencing and so on. The drying bundles of stems make good hiding places for much wildlife.

As Robinson realized, the light in a coppice enables a rich underplanting. In earliest spring, the catkins expand at the same time as pale blue *Scilla mischtschenkoana* flowers. The combination is very pretty. The sweet box (*Sarcococca humilis*) planted by the seat will still be in flower and will perfume the chilly air. The planting is continued with drifts of one of the blue pulmonarias, dog's-tooth violets, plain honest bluebells and more.

The planting of bulbs and other woodlanders is intended to become a closed carpet of greenery. Everything needs to be planted in ground cleared of grasses and weeds. The plants will take two or three seasons to become dense enough to repel invasion, and need to be weeded until then. If you want a faster effect, double up the quantities.

The pool margin is decorated with wild flag iris; this could be the pale cream form, with slightly larger flowers than the wildling, called *Iris pseudacorus* var. *bastardii*. However suspect its parentage, it seeds easily and prolifically. There will soon be a stand of it to rival anything in local wetlands. The iris also has a double form, which contrives to look merely muddled. My favourite choice would be the splendid hybrid between the wild flag and the Chinese *Iris chrysographes* called *I. x robusta* 'Holden Clough'. Its tawny yellow petals are extraordinarily netted with purplish brown lines; sinister but handsome.

The flower borders near the house are filled with plants that Robinson liked. He let the red valerian (*Centranthus ruber*) seed where it liked – even into his walls and balustrades, which looks attractive, but isn't good for the architectural fabric. Otherwise, the borders need the usual maintenance of all flower beds, and they will give you something beautiful to look at in their second season of tenure, whilst the coppice is still growing.

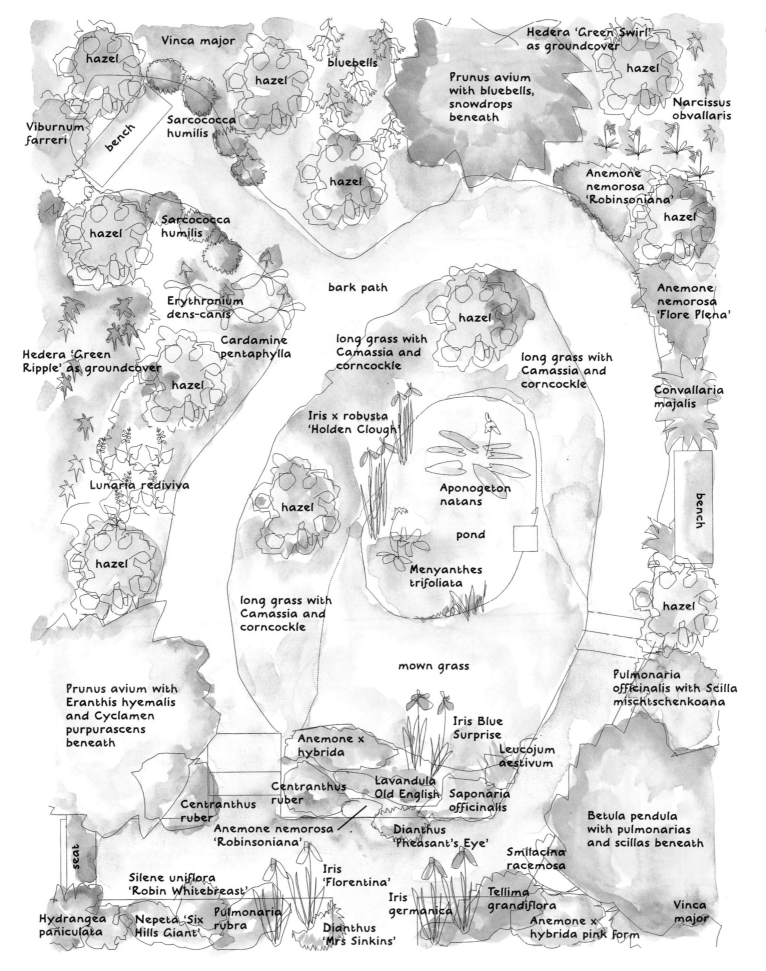

hazel

Vinca major

bluebells

Hedera 'Green Swirl' as groundcover

hazel

Viburnum farreri

bench

Sarcococca humilis

hazel

Prunus avium with bluebells, snowdrops beneath

Narcissus obvallaris

hazel

Anemone nemorosa 'Robinsoniana'

hazel

Sarcococca humilis

hazel

bark path

hazel

Anemone nemorosa 'Flore Plena'

Erythronium dens-canis

long grass with Camassia and corncockle

long grass with Camassia and corncockle

Hedera 'Green Ripple' as groundcover

Cardamine pentaphylla

hazel

Convallaria majalis

Iris x robusta 'Holden Clough'

Lunaria rediviva

hazel

Aponogeton natans

pond

bench

hazel

hazel

Menyanthes trifoliata

long grass with Camassia and corncockle

hazel

mown grass

Pulmonaria officinalis with Scilla mischtschenkoana

Prunus avium with Eranthis hyemalis and Cyclamen purpurascens beneath

Anemone x hybrida

Iris Blue Surprise

Centranthus ruber

Leucojum aestivum

Lavandula Old English

Saponaria officinalis

Centranthus ruber

Betula pendula with pulmonarias and scillas beneath

Anemone nemorosa 'Robinsoniana'

Dianthus 'Pheasant's Eye'

seat

Smilacina racemosa

Silene uniflora 'Robin Whitebreast'

Iris 'Florentina'

Iris germanica

Tellima grandiflora

Vinca major

Hydrangea paniculata

Nepeta 'Six Hills Giant'

Pulmonaria rubra

Dianthus 'Mrs Sinkins'

Anemone x hybrida pink form

SHOPPING LIST

AQUATIC PLANTING

2 *Aponogeton natans*

3 *Menyanthes trifoliata*

BULBS

150 *Hyacinthoides non-scripta* (bluebells)

25 *Camassia leichtlinii*

50 *Cyclamen purpurascens*

200 *Eranthis hyemalis*

50 *Erythronium dens-canis*

200 *Galanthus nivalis* (snowdrops)

50 *Leucojum aestivum*

100 *Narcissus obvallaris*

100 *Scilla mischtschenkoana*

HERBACEOUS PLANTING

50 *Anemone nemorosa* 'Robinsoniana'

50 *Anemone nemorosa* 'Flore Pleno'

6 *Anemone x hybrida*

6 *Anemone x hybrida* pink form

6 *Cardamine pentaphylla*

50 *Convallaria majalis*

3 *Dianthus* 'Mrs Sinkins'

3 *Dianthus* 'Pheasant's Eye'

6 *Iris* Blue Surprise

6 *Iris* 'Florentina'

6 *Iris germanica*

3 *Iris x robusta* 'Holden Clough'

50 *Hedera helix* 'Green Ripple'

6 *Nepeta* 'Six Hills Giant'

6 *Pulmonaria officinalis*

6 *Pulmonaria rubra*

3 *Saponaria officinalis*

6 *Silene uniflora* 'Robin Whitebreast'

3 *Smilacina racemosa*

6 *Tellima grandiflora*

50 *Vinca major*

SEED

corncockle

Centranthus ruber

Lunaria rediviva

SHRUBS

1 *Hydrangea paniculata*

9 *Lavandula x intermedia* Old English Group

8 *Sarcococca humilis*

2 *Viburnum farreri*

TREES

1 *Betula pendula*

2 *Prunus avium* (bird cherry)

9 *Corylus* (hazel) varieties (see page 64)

Left: *Centranthus ruber*

Opposite top left: *Anemone x hybrida* pink form

Opposite top centre: *Eranthis hyemalis*

Opposite top right: *Hyacinthoides non-scripta*

Opposite centre left: *Iris x robusta* 'Holden Clough'

Opposite centre: *Erythronium dens-canis*

Opposite centre right: *Corylus avellana*

Opposite bottom: *Camassia leichtlinii*

AN EDWARDIAN COLOUR BORDER

GERTRUDE JEYKLL AT MUNSTEAD WOOD

GERTRUDE JEKYLL (1843–1932) trained as a painter (at the Kensington School of Art), and though, in her thirties, her eyesight became so poor that she could no longer function as an artist and craftswoman, her 'inner eye' never left her. Like many rather wealthy and very independent ladies of the day, she was fascinated by gardens and plants. She could write easily and persuasively, so the stage was set for her to become a major figure on the gardening scene. She was also good at meeting influential men. She became associated with William Robinson and his magazines, and she absorbed his ideas about how plantings should be made. He gave her a platform on which to expound her novel ideas about the possibility of using the colour of herbaceous plant flowers in ways that an artist would, ways that were far removed from the brash clash of scarlet, yellow and blue then thought of as the only colour scheme worth having in the bedding garden. When she decided to have her own substantial house built, she chose the young Edwin Lutyens as architect. Lutyens shared her love of the 16th- and 17th-century farmhouses of the Sussex countryside. Her new house, Munstead Wood, used the vernacular idiom, combined with the conveniences and conventions of prosperous late-19th-century living. She and Lutyens developed a close friendship, and together designed many house-and-garden schemes of great finesse.

One of her key contributions to gardening was her use of colour in developing the herbaceous border. Gardeners were getting tired of the huge expanses of dwarfed, if colourful, plants used in bedding schemes. They wanted lupins and tall delphiniums, big poppies, lilies, purple eupatoriums and more. She realized that these could be used in painterly ways, making handsome, often very clever, colour schemes along the length of the whole border. Her liking for architectural simplicity meant that her borders were often long rectangles, backed by brick walls or yew hedges. However, working in her own time and class, she could always assume a good supply of garden staff. She had, at times, fourteen gardeners working at Munstead Wood, though some of these were employed in her plant nursery, which supplied the emerging market with many lovely new plants.

An arched doorway in an old stone wall offers an enticing glimpse through to more of the garden at Munstead Wood. The foreground planting of sedums, geraniums and asters, tied together with silver foliage, is an echoing memory of the subtle plantings that Gertrude Jekyll designed for Munstead, which she often used as a trial ground for new plants and new planting ideas.

Her influence is still very strong, and much of her powerfully evocative writing is still in print – books like the enchanting *Wood and Garden* and *Colour in the Flower Garden*. The Jekyll gardens at Hestercombe (Somerset) and Upton Grey (Hampshire), and her own much-loved garden at Munstead Wood in Surrey are all being restored.

NOTES ON THE PLAN

This is almost exactly one of Miss Jekyll's own plans, much smaller than her usual ones, and carried out in many shades of blue, from the deep purple of the eupatoriums to the blazing sapphire of the phacelias, and set off with greenish yellows from the rues (*Ruta graveolens*), the tall *Thalictrum flavum* and the floppy

clematis species, soft yellows from the snapdragons, sharp yellow from *Lilium monadelphum* (syn. *L. szovitsianum*), and plenty of white. She often used the variegated form of maize (*Zea mays*) to act as a visual 'blender' for the whole scheme. Some of the plants she used are now no longer commercially available. The plan suggests plants as similar as possible that can still easily be found.

The season will run from early summer into autumn. Miss Jekyll kept a glasshouse and frame bed filled with pots of lilies, tobaccos, stocks and more, so that if gaps developed in the flowering of the borders, the potted plants could be slipped into the vacant spaces. As this is an important aspect of her borders, and essential if a herbaceous border is to take up the

whole garden, the plan shows a service area tucked away behind a hedge.

The plan adds two beds to the full Jekyll scheme. These are for the rose 'The Garland' that Jekyll loved; she had this vigorous climber growing along the walls of Munstead Wood. Its amethyst-flushed white flowers will delight you for many weeks of early summer. Support on tall pyramids of wooden poles.

BUILDING IT

It is useful to have the garden framed by hedges. Yew is specified in the shopping list; faster-growing plants like privet or *Lonicera nitida* are as good, but only if they are well maintained. Most hedge plants are greedy feeders, and the grass path at the back of the

The paintings below are taken from Some English Gardens *(first published in 1904) by Gertrude Jekyll and the artist George Elgood (1851–1943), who specialized in garden paintings and often illustrated Miss Jekyll's work. 'Ramscliffe: larkspur' (below left) is a planting she admired, in which campanulas, delphiniums, helianthus and* Stachys lanata *combine in a colour scheme very similar in content to her plan given here with only the most minor adaptations. 'Michaelmas daisies at Munstead Wood' (below right) shows her using aster hybrids in various sizes and colours in her own garden. Many of her varieties are now lost, but modern ones can be used in entirely comparable ways and to similar effect.*

flower beds is as much to stop them draining the beds of nutrients as it is to help maintain the flowers. They also give splendid cross-views of the garden.

The seat would most happily be one of those loosely called 'Lutyens' seats, though his design owes much to those shown in 18th-century prints of Chiswick House near London, which were themselves probably copied from Chinese designs. Paint it a classic green or deep blue.

The sundial should be as large as possible, and on a plinth wide enough to place clusters of pots of scented-leaf geraniums, and perhaps one or two with magenta flowers. Jekyll also liked pots of *Francoa sonchifolia*, with its long wands of pale pink flowers. It is easily grown from seed.

PLANTING AND MAINTAINING IT

Most herbaceous plants are greedy for nutrients, so ensure that the ground is in good shape before planting. As almost all the plants will be containerized, they can be planted as and when they become available. In their first season, the colour will be thin. The second season will be good, and the third splendid. Miss Jekyll had plenty of labour to clear away the dead stems late in each autumn. This isn't essential, and indeed a frost-rimed tangle of stems can be good to look at. In very early spring, most of the dried stuff is easily raked off with a lawn rake. More resistant stems are easily cut or strimmed down and removed. Herbaceous borders produce copious debris which needs composting. The compost should be returned to the beds when it is ready. This will make a huge difference to the plants.

Jekyll's gardeners would also have spent plenty of time putting in supporting canes for the delphiniums, maize plants, hollyhocks and more. The eupatoriums and thalictrums are self-supporting. Young cats seem especially attracted to the idea of clambering up maize stems – something the cat-loving Miss Jekyll might

well have seen. The clematis species are all scramblers, and need pyramids of branches perhaps a yard high to support them. Some plants of *Clematis recta* have a delicious smell. The white perennial pea can be supported in the same way, though she may have intended them to scramble prettily through the purple-flowered eupatoriums.

The lilies, and certainly *Lilium longiflorum*, may need lifting over winter. All last well in pots, so it is worth merely sinking the pots in the ground in spring. *Lilium longiflorum* can be found in short-stemmed forms which will vanish amongst everything else; the planting requires the tall ones that can get to 1.5m/5ft or so, and can need staking. If you can't find the right sort, use the pure white form of *Lilum regale*, or *L. candidum*. Both are hardy.

Also from the greenhouse, Miss Jekyll used *Plumbago auriculata* (syn. *P. capensis*) with its lovely china blue flowers. It will need to be lifted and rehoused before the first heavy frosts. Frozen ground will also kill off *Salvia patens*. If you want to chance it, you can leave it in the ground and save plenty of the large black seed it produces freely. Alternatively, the roots are substantial and easily lifted; store the plants somewhere dry and frost free.

After five or six seasons, the hollyhocks, delphiniums and lupins will need renewing. The eupatoriums will have become too domineering, so dig them up, divide them and replant a few divisions in each original site.

Lastly, pests and diseases. The hostas Jekyll suggests are not as attractive to snails as some in the genus, but it is worth scattering slug bait around them to keep the leaves in perfect shape. Slugs will wreck the perennial delphiniums, too, in early spring, unless the plants are heavily protected. The hollyhocks may suffer from rust fungus, shown as small orange spots on distorted leaves. Spray, and, the following season, spray fortnightly as soon as growth shows.

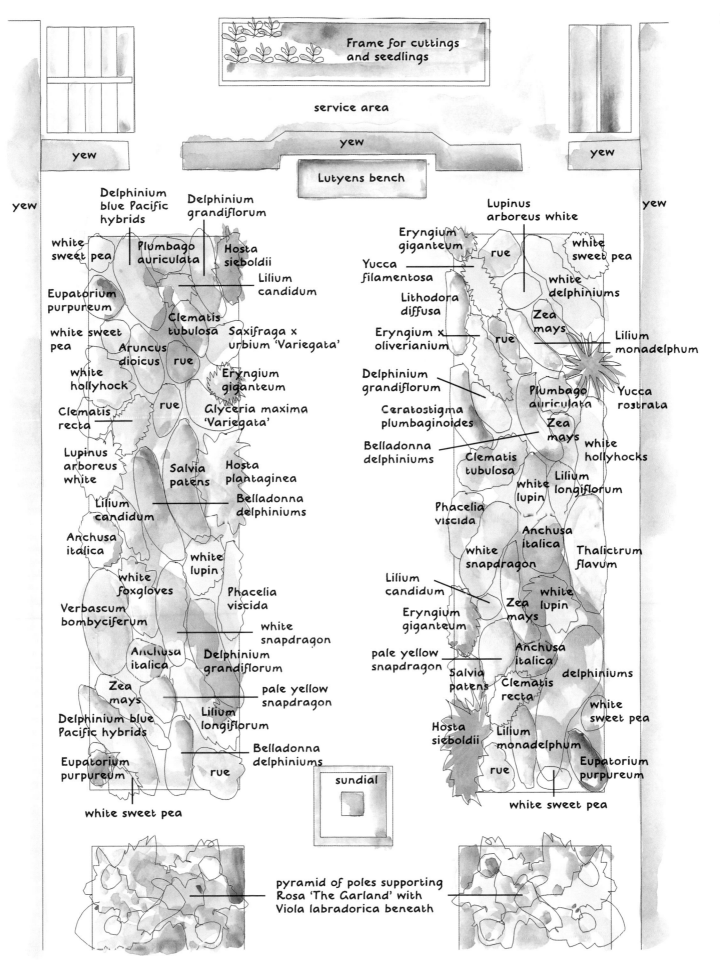

Frame for cuttings and seedlings

service area

yew

yew

Lutyens bench

yew

yew

yew

yew

Delphinium blue Pacific hybrids

Delphinium grandiflorum

white sweet pea

Plumbago auriculata

Hosta sieboldii

Lilium candidum

Eupatorium purpureum

white sweet pea

Clematis tubulosa

Saxifraga x urbium 'Variegata'

Aruncus dioicus

rue

white hollyhock

Eryngium giganteum

Clematis recta

rue

Glyceria maxima 'Variegata'

Lupinus arboreus white

Salvia patens

Hosta plantaginea

Lilium candidum

Belladonna delphiniums

Anchusa italica

white lupin

white foxgloves

Phacelia viscida

Verbascum bombyciferum

white snapdragon

Anchusa italica

Delphinium grandiflorum

Zea mays

pale yellow snapdragon

Delphinium blue Pacific hybrids

Lilium longiflorum

Eupatorium purpureum

rue

Belladonna delphiniums

white sweet pea

Lupinus arboreus white

Eryngium giganteum

Yucca filamentosa

rue

white sweet pea

white delphiniums

Lithodora diffusa

Zea mays

Eryngium x oliverianum

rue

Lilium monadelphum

Delphinium grandiflorum

Plumbago auriculata

Yucca rostrata

Ceratostigma plumbaginoides

Zea mays

Belladonna delphiniums

Clematis tubulosa

white hollyhocks

white lupin

Lilium longiflorum

Phacelia viscida

Anchusa italica

Thalictrum flavum

white snapdragon

Lilium candidum

Zea mays

white lupin

Eryngium giganteum

pale yellow snapdragon

Anchusa italica

delphiniums

Salvia patens

Clematis recta

white sweet pea

Hosta sieboldii

Lilium monadelphum

Eupatorium purpureum

rue

white sweet pea

sundial

pyramid of poles supporting Rosa 'The Garland' with Viola labradorica beneath

SHOPPING LIST

BULBS

12 *Lilium candidum*

6 *Lilium longiflorum*

6 *Lilium monadelphum* (syn. *L. szovitsianum*)

HERBACEOUS PLANTING

3 *Aruncus dioicus*

6 *Ceratostigma plumbaginoides*

12 *Delphinium,* white

12 *Delphinium,* miscellaneous blues

6 *Eryngium x oliverianum*

3 *Eupatorium purpureum*

1 *Glyceria maxima* var. *variegata*

3 *Hosta plantaginea*

6 *Hosta sieboldii*

3 *Lithodora diffusa*

12 *Lupinus,* white

6 *Lupinus arboreus* (tree lupins), white

6 *Plumbago auriculata*

18 *Salvia patens*

6 *Saxifraga x urbium* 'Variegata'

6 *Thalictrum flavum*

24 *Viola labradorica*

1 *Yucca filamentosa*

1 *Yucca rostrata*

ROSES

2 *Rosa* 'The Garland'

SEED

18 *Alcea rosea* (hollyhocks), white

24 *Anchusa italica*

18 *Antirrhinum majus* (snapdragon), white

24 *Antirrhinum majus* (snapdragon), pale yellow

24 *Delphinium* Belladona Group

1pkt *Delphinium grandiflorum*

12 *Delphinium* Pacific hybrids, blue

1pkt *Digitalis purpurea* 'Alba' (white foxgloves)

18 *Eryngium giganteum*

18 *Lathyrus* (sweet pea), white

1pkt *Phacelia viscida*

6 *Verbascum bombyciferum*

36 *Zea mays,* variegated

SHRUBS

4 *Clematis tubulosa* (syn *C. davidiana*)

2 *Clematis recta*

18 *Ruta graveolens* (rue)

TREES

250 *Taxus baccata*

Opposite: Blue delphinium hybrids
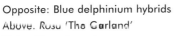Above: Rosa 'The Garland'
Right: *Clematis recta*
Below left: *Salvia patens*
Below centre: *Eryngium giganteum*
Below right: *Lilium candidum*

A MONET WATER GARDEN

CLAUDE MONET AT GIVERNY

Now fully restored, Claude Monet's garden at Giverny in Normandy is both famous and beautiful. Monet, who gardened there from 1883, was an avant garde gardener as well as an adventurous artist. By 1895 he was becoming successful, and bought an extra piece of ground that had a small stream running through it. He wanted to grow some of the exciting plants that were then just appearing in gardens – especially some sumptuous new waterlilies. These were crosses between hardy European and American species, and tropical ones from the jungles of South America and Asia. Bred by a French enthusiast called M. Latour-Marliac, they caused a sensation. Monet had to have them, so he dammed his stream, created lakes and filled them with these beautiful water plants. He was so enthralled by his waterlilies that many of his later paintings were vast, dreamlike meditations on their beauty.

Monet ringed his water garden with weeping willows (*Salix babylonica* var. *pekinensis* 'Pendula') and Lombardy poplars (*Populus nigra* 'Italica'). He planted the margins of the lake with great clumps of the newly imported Japanese irises and hostas, as well as more familiar plants like skunk cabbage (*Lysichiton americanus*), Siberian iris, ferns and sedges. These are all included in the plan.

NOTES ON THE PLAN

Monet had plenty of space for pavilions and forest trees as well as water, but smaller gardens can contain as much magic if the pond forms the whole central zone of the plot. The delight of Giverny is the contrast of the horizontal plane of water and lily leaves with the luxuriant background planting of willows and poplars. However, waterlilies need plenty of sunlight to flower well, and so here, where large trees would quickly throw everything else into shadow, the garden plan uses bamboos to provide the vertical lines

Much of the drama at Giverny comes from the contrast of horizontal and vertical elements. In a small space, irises, bamboos and grasses can replace the weeping willows. Their stems and reflections will counterpoint the horizontal rafts of waterlilies.

of the willows, and oriental cherry and maple species to make lovely but small-scale stand-ins for the poplars.

The Monet scene, though so famously based on waterlilies, is dependent on a much wider range of plants, both at the water's edge and beyond. The plan shows a fairly complex planting scheme at the water's edge, sometimes using tall plants to stop the whole garden being seen at once. It contains plenty of good, contrasting foliage; too much flower colour will take the eye away from the waterlilies. The planting on the margins of the garden is simpler, but will still give a good long season of interest, including perfume and autumn colour. Once mature, it will also screen off the outside world without cutting out too much light.

Monet created not only handsome plantings but also places from which to view them. Bridges, pergolas, even lovely green-painted punts, all add to the Giverny atmosphere. Here, the pergola is an essential element in the re-creation. In the plan, it is attached to a summerhouse, but it could easily cover the entire corner of the garden, and would make a lovely place in which to sit during the wisteria's season of flower. Paint the structure viridian green. If you need a longer season of flower, you could add a climbing rose. Avoid clematis; the foliage will soon be so dense that the wisteria will die out.

BUILDING IT

The Giverny water garden was created from flat waterlogged ground. Few small gardens are so

Right: The Japanese passion for wisterias reached Europe as part of the European obsession for Japan amongst artists and the artistic during the latter part of the 19th century; Monet, an enthusiast too, used wisterias to add oriental reflections to his pools.

Far right: The marginal waterside plantings at Giverny are quite as handsome as those of the open water, though much less well known. Here, asclepias, tagetes and nicotianas look splendid surrounding a clump of Iris pseudacorus.

fortunate, but modern plastics allow any reasonably flat garden to have a good-sized pool. Many waterlilies only need 50cm/20in depth of water, and even the largest sorts will grow well in only twice that. The area of the pool needs to be large enough to accommodate at least six large patches of waterlilies and so should be around 18.5m²/200ft² in area.

The plan makes use of an L-shaped pool; with irregular marginal areas disguising the basic shape, there are interesting views from different parts of the garden. The marginal plants need damp ground. You can create it by setting their soil over additional sheeting, or by manipulating the pool's excavations so that there is a shallow lip around the margin. However, either of those methods means that the marginal plants have a limited amount of soil in which to grow. It is best if you can plant the marginals in open ground, and ensure that there is enough overflow from the pool to keep their roots constantly moist. Their exuberant growth will swiftly cover the awkward margins of the pool, where the butyl liner comes to the surface. The shopping list suggests plant numbers to give a reasonably filled look to the garden in two or three seasons.

In warm or subtropical gardens, the waterlilies could include 'Saint Louis Gold' (lemon gold, scented), 'Virginia' (white), 'Blue Beauty' (blue) or 'Sunrise' (yellow). The Giverny pool sometimes has other aquatics like *Potamogeton* and *Aponogeton*, though these are invasive and need to be heavily controlled. *Aponogeton* is good by a terrace or seating area, as the flowers have a delectable smell, especially in the morning. Avoid species of duckweed. They rapidly cover the water surface, killing reflections and shading out pond life and the young lily growth.

Only the largest garden and pool can manage a proper bridge. The essence of the feature, though, is its colour and the abundance of the wisterias it supports. Here, a simple pergola makes an enchanting reflection. Alternatively, copy the structure in the main photograph; it is only a simple series of arches made of metal tubing, generously

sized to arch over a couple of garden seats. Plant it with a rose like 'The Garland' or 'Janet B. Wood', if you don't want to use wisteria.

Paths can be of mown grass, though a more solid material is far better. Paths at Giverny are of rolled fine-grade river gravel, bound with sand. In a small garden, coarse sand, 7cm/3in deep over nylon landscape sheeting, is fine.

PLANTING AND MAINTAINING IT

The main problem with modern pools created using butyl sheeting is the way that the margin is treated. It must be concealed by the plantings and not emphasized by rows of pebbles. The hostas, rodgersias, ferns and sedges shown in the plan are especially good for this. The edge of the pond also needs to be steep so that the water gets deep as soon as possible. This makes the sheeting less visible in winter when the water is clear. Against the terrace and the 'bridge', the sheeting is easily tucked underneath the hard edge of each built area.

Many landscape contractors will suggest that you add some sort of filtration system. Monet's pools have no such thing, and are often fairly green with algae. In any case, crystal-clear water merely gives a good view of how the pool is built, something to forget. Add fish. Frogs and newts may colonize of their own accord. Dragonflies and damselflies will soon appear. The pool will balance itself in a natural way, and the waterlilies will soon float their marvellous flowers on its surface. With no natural water source and vigorous plantings, the water will gradually evaporate during the growing season. An easy supply needs to be on hand. Once the pool has achieved a balance of animal and plant life, the spring growth of algae will be naturally controlled.

Maintenance of the other plants is the same as for any garden. Don't be tempted to plant bamboos too close to the pool's edge; they 'run' and the new shoots can pierce the sheeting with great ease. Although the junction can be reasonably watertight, when the stem rots or is pulled out, the hole will leak water. Eradicate moles. They can easily tunnel through pool liner.

Top: *Nymphaea 'Marliacea Chromatella'*
Above: *Nymphaea 'Marliacea Albida'*
Below: *Nymphaea 'Vésuve'*

SHOPPING LIST

WATERLILIES

1 *Nymphaea 'Caroliniana'*
1 *Nymphaea 'Escarboucle'*
1 *Nymphaea 'Froebelii'*
1 *Nymphaea 'Marliacea Albida'*
1 *Nymphaea 'Marliacea Chromatella'*
1 *Nymphaea 'Vésuve'*

HERBACEOUS PLANTING

5 *Aconitum carmichaelii*
6 *Anemone x hybrida 'Honorine Jobert'*
8 *Anemone x hybrida 'Whirlwind'*
12 *Aruncus dioicus*
6 *Astilbe x arendsii 'Irrlicht'*
6 *Bergenia 'Brahms'*
12 *Brunnera macrophylla 'Langtrees'*
5 *Carex aurea*
6 *Convallaria majalis*
5 *Dicentra spectabilis*
3 *Euphorbia palustris*
6 *Hedera helix 'Parsley Crested'*
3 *Hemerocallis fulva*
3 *Hemerocallis lilioasphodelus*
3 *Iris pseudacorus 'Variegata'*
4 *Ligularia dentata 'Desdemona'*
1 *Macleaya cordata*
8 *Meconopsis betonicifolia*
3 *Milium effusum 'Aureum'*
5 *Polygonatum x hybridum*
6 *Polystichum setiferum*
12 *Viola labradorica*

MARGINAL PLANTING

5 *Astilbe x arendsii 'Lilli Goos'*
1 *Astilboides tabularis*
3 *Carex aurea*
1 *Carex comans 'Bronze'*
3 *Darmera peltata*
7 *Heuchera hispida*
3 each *Hosta 'Krossa Regal'* and *'Royal Standard'*
3 *Hosta sieboldii*
3 *Hosta tokudama*

5 *Houttuynia cordata*

3 *Iris ensata* 'Chiyo-no-haru'

3 *Iris ensata* 'Suwagoryo'

3 *Iris sibirica* 'Ego'

3 *Iris sibirica* 'Peaches and Cream'

4 *Ligularia dentata* 'Desdemona'

3 *Lysichiton americanus*

5 *Matteuccia struthiopteris*

3 *Mimulus cardinalis*

3 *Mimulus moschatus*

5 *Onoclea sensibilis*

3 *Osmunda regalis*

5 *Paeonia lactiflora* 'Bowl of Beauty'

5 *Persicaria milettii*

5 *Phragmites communis*

6 *Primula florindae*

9 *Pulmonaria rubra*

6 *Rodgersia aesculifolia*

3 *Rodgersia pinnata*

SHRUBS

1 *Camellia japonica* 'Gloire de Nantes'

1 *Clematis montana*

5 *Hedera helix* 'Parsley Crested'

3 *Lonicera periclymenum* 'Serotina'

1 *Philadelphus* 'Manteau d'Hermine'

1 *Phyllostachys nigra*

1 *Pseudosasa japonica*

3 *Rhododendron luteum*

1 *Rosa* 'Souvenir de la Malmaison'

3 *Sasa veitchii*

3 *Skimmia japonica*

1 *Spiraea henryi*

TREES

4 *Acer tataricum* subsp. *ginnala*

1 *Acer japonicum* 'Vitifolium'

1 *Magnolia salicifolia* 'Wada's Memory'

2 *Prunus sargentii*

1 *Prunus x subhirtella* 'Autumnalis'

1 *Syringa vulgaris* 'Madame F. Morel'

1 *Syringa vulgaris* 'Andenken an Ludwig Späth'

1 *Viburnum x bodnantense* 'Dawn'

2 *Wisteria sinensis* 'Prolific'

Top left: *Lysichiton americanus*
Top right: *Primula florindae*
Below: *Philadelphus* 'Manteau d'Hermine'
Bottom: *Hemerocallis lilioasphodelus*

A WORLD OF ROSES

JULES GRAVEREAUX'S
ROSERAIE DE L'HAY

I N 1899, a successful French businessman, already in love with the rose, decided to devote his retirement to growing them. As he was Jules Gravereaux, and owned the famous Paris department store Bon Marché, his garden was going to be special: it was going to grow every rose in existence. Though even Roman gardeners had had a couple of gorgeous double roses, which are still grown, it was only in the late 18th century that hundreds of new varieties began to appear. They combined the ancient garden roses of Europe and the Middle East with new species recently introduced to Europe from America, India and China. European gardens were soon flooded with wondrous new things. Empress Josephine, wife of Napoleon, became a great enthusiast and created a famous rose garden at Malmaison. Fashionable gardeners all over Europe, and also in North America, had to have rose gardens. Though new hybrids appeared wherever roses were grown, it was through Josephine's encouragement that French breeders remained the most important producers of new roses until quite recent times, when American, British and German breeders eclipsed them.

Gravereaux's new garden, designed with the help of architect Eduard André, was to show how roses evolved, how variable they were and how they should be grown. The garden, called Roseraie de l'Haÿ, soon became a sensational success, and remains one of the most important collections of roses in the world, nowadays containing well over three thousand varieties and species.

NOTES ON THE PLAN
The Roseraie de l'Haÿ was, when planned, only part of a very large estate. Many of the roses that Gravereaux grew had just a single burst of flowers, but for him it didn't matter that once the roses were over, there wasn't much to see. Nowadays, there are many more varieties that flower from

This wonderful sequence of roses slung nonchalantly over their arches at Roseraie de l'Haÿ shows the advantage of growing roses and other flowering climbers on arches rather than over long pergolas or tunnels: individual plants get much more light, and so will flower at the sides and underneath.

early summer well into autumn, so it is possible to have a whole garden devoted solely to the rose. There are, though, so many marvels amongst the short-season roses that just have to be grown that a peak from late June to the end of July is both inevitable and wonderful.

The plan is based on the section of Roseraie de l'Haÿ devoted to French roses of the mid- and late 19th century, whose design harked back to the 17th century, the golden age of French garden design. The plan has two sections; in the pool garden, the roses are mostly hybrids involving the Japanese *Rosa rugosa*. They flower well for most of the season, often smell wonderful and need very little in the way of maintenance. Most have been bred since Gravereaux's death in 1916; one of the most gorgeous is even named after the garden. The first section contains some of the loveliest 'old' shrub roses, most of which flower in late June and early July, though some will go on flowering, if less powerfully, into August.

The plan covers the rose arches with climbing roses that often have a much longer season. The marvellous amethyst pink, and American-bred, hybrid 'Noisette Carnée' (sometimes called 'Blush Noisette') keeps

flowering well into early winter. 'Madame Alfred Carrière' will often do the same, so the rose arches will give pleasure until then.

BUILDING IT

Apart from the roses themselves, the key element in this garden is trelliswork. Parts of the Roseraie de l'Haÿ imitate the great trellis architecture of French gardens in the early 17th century. The plan merely suggests you try a pavilion in both distant corners of the garden, and enclose the garden with a trellis boundary 2m/6½ft high on which to drape the white *Rosa* 'City of York' (now, correctly, 'Direktör Benschop'). Trellis needs painting; oil-based paints are best, though they need reapplying every couple of seasons. White is too glaring; mid or dark blues or greens set off the roses exceptionally well.

The most vital elements of all in the design are the rose arches. Few of the cheaper commercial arches are sufficiently wide, or even high. Good copies of 19th-century designs can be found, but it may be simpler to make, or have made, stout supports using 10 x 10cm/ 4 x 4in posts as uprights, joining them with strong horizontal posts to make pergolas rather than arches.

*Left: The pool is
surrounded by an
overwhelming amount of
flowers, many of the plants
being trained over the
grand and elaborate trellis
arbours. The central
domed pavilion, flanked
by arcades, was based on
arbours popular in French
gardens of the 17th and
18th centuries. In the
plan, two small trellis
arbours are suggested.*

*Right: The grand trellis
pavilion and arcades at
Roseraie de l'Haÿ are
covered in the beautiful
dark pink blooms of the
long-stemmed and
vigorous rambler
'Alexandre Girault'.*

They would also be perfectly in keeping with late-19th-century style. They do have to be strong; the vegetation can be heavy, and if you don't manage to thin the rose stems every two or three seasons, the weight of rose will eventually overwhelm the stoutest support. Height too is important, for the roses will, even when tied in carefully, hang somewhat from the crossbars. The minimum height for a rose arch is about 2.5m/8ft.

The advantage of a series of arches over long pergolas or tunnels is that the individual plants get much more light, and so will flower at the sides and underneath. Roses (and any other plant) grown on pergolas and tunnels flower mostly on the uppermost, and largely unseen, surface.

Paths at Roseraie de l'Haÿ are of gravel or brick, with low box or brick edgings. In a garden as densely planted as that in the plan, brick is preferable. Fallen flowers and petals are more easily swept away.

As in the French garden, a broad pool reflects the trellis arcades and pavilion that support huge swathes of the rose 'Alexandre Girault'. In the plan, this rambler is planted on two corner trellis arbours, and the small pool is partly edged with the low-growing rose 'De Meaux', its flowers deep burgundy and well scented. A central urn, dripping water from its fluted edges, would make a good 19th-century touch.

If you don't want the expense of a pool, a circle of grass will also look good. The centrepiece could be an urn, or a very large pot, perhaps filled with the enchanting, and only half-hardy, Chinese garden rose often called, in the West, 'Old Blush China' (correctly, it is R. x odorata 'Pallida'). Extremely pretty in its own right, and flowering all through the growing season, it is of great historical significance, being the provider of the long flowering season to many modern roses. It will flower all winter under glass. Ideally, the pavilions should be made of painted trelliswork and be large enough to enclose some comfortable seating – a bench or some chairs. Alternatively, one or both could be garden sheds, suitably decorated and rose-covered.

PLANTING AND MAINTAINING IT

Most of the rose varieties suggested are widely available. Alternatively, substitute roses of your choice. Keep the colour range limited; a tumble of yellow, pink, orange, scarlet, and so on, can look busy and spotty. Some gardeners don't like the shortness of season of the 'old' roses, and plant the so-called English roses. These do indeed have a long season, and are moderately pretty. None has either the delicacy of form and colour, or the often ravishing smell, of the old sorts.

If you don't like bare earth beneath roses, I find Viola cornuta varieties look splendid, as do some of the grander Viola hybrids: 'Maggie Mott' and 'Vita', in silvery mauves and rose purples, are especially good. Pulmonarias and periwinkles always seem to do well too. Add bulbs for spring, particularly the early Scilla mischtschenkoana and forms of Narcissus triandrus. For late summer and autumn, Schizostylis and hardy agapanthus are excellent.

The shrub roses need little work. Thin out the tangle every few seasons. Some, depending on the location, can get spindly and floppy. Give them support, perhaps a low pyramid of wooden poles. Some are subject to blackspot, particularly 'Madame Alfred Carrière' and Rosa gallica 'Versicolor'; it probably won't be possible to spray the climbers, but the bushes are easily looked after. Once the garden is established, the rose chafer bug will gradually build up. It eats the heart out of each bud, and you may need to start spraying the bushes once a fortnight as the buds begin to show.

The climbers are all enthusiastic growers, and will soon get overwhelmingly large. Thin out entire stems from the base of the plant every second season or so. This is most easily done if the rose is untied from the arch. If the tangle is simply too much, it is best to cut the entire plant back to a couple of feet from the root, and start again.

Most of the roses suggested are hardy, though in my present garden (in southern Scotland) 'Noisette Carnée' is sometimes killed to ground level.

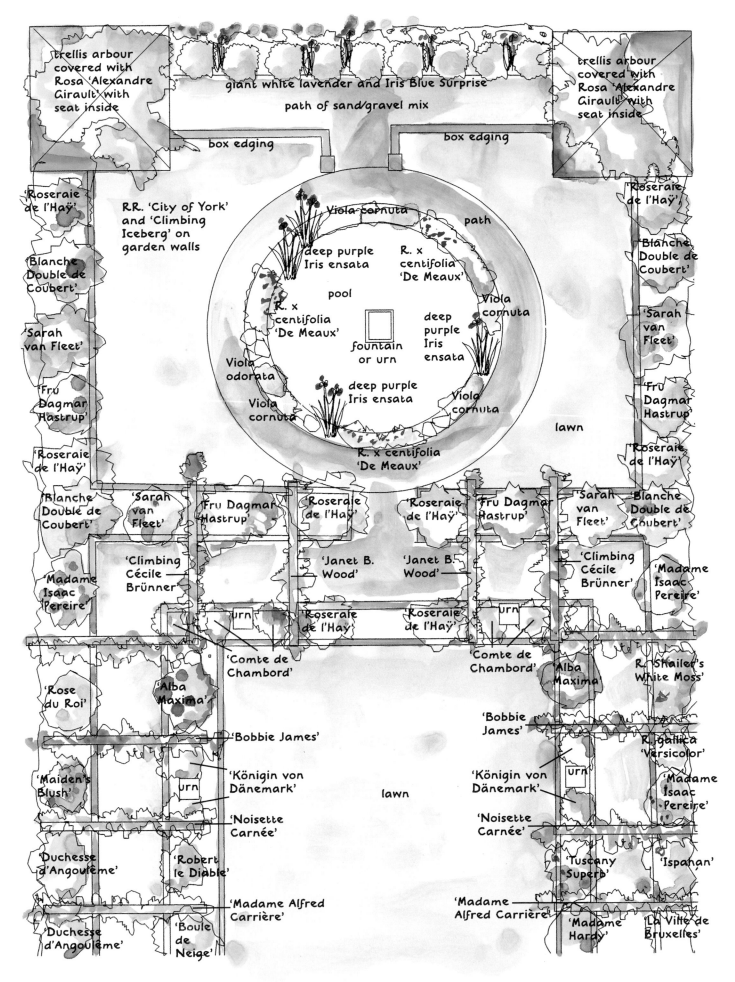

trellis arbour covered with Rosa 'Alexandre Girault' with seat inside

giant white lavender and Iris Blue Surprise

path of sand/gravel mix

trellis arbour covered with Rosa 'Alexandre Girault' with seat inside

box edging

box edging

'Roseraie de l'Haÿ'

'Roseraie de l'Haÿ'

R.R. 'City of York' and 'Climbing Iceberg' on garden walls

Viola cornuta

path

'Blanche Double de Coubert'

'Blanche Double de Coubert'

deep purple Iris ensata

R. x centifolia 'De Meaux'

'Sarah van Fleet'

R. x centifolia 'De Meaux'

pool

Viola cornuta

'Sarah van Fleet'

'Fru Dagmar Hastrup'

fountain or urn

deep purple Iris ensata

'Fru Dagmar Hastrup'

Viola odorata

'Roseraie de l'Haÿ'

deep purple Iris ensata

lawn

'Roseraie de l'Haÿ'

Viola cornuta

Viola cornuta

R. x centifolia 'De Meaux'

'Blanche Double de Coubert'

'Sarah van Fleet'

'Fru Dagmar Hastrup'

'Roseraie de l'Haÿ'

'Roseraie de l'Haÿ'

'Fru Dagmar Hastrup'

'Sarah van Fleet'

'Blanche Double de Coubert'

'Climbing Cécile Brünner'

'Janet B. Wood'

'Janet B. Wood'

'Climbing Cécile Brünner'

'Madame Isaac Pereire'

'Madame Isaac Pereire'

urn

'Roseraie de l'Haÿ'

'Roseraie de l'Haÿ'

urn

'Comte de Chambord'

'Comte de Chambord'

Alba Maxima

R. Shailer's White Moss'

'Rose du Roi'

'Alba Maxima'

'Bobbie James'

'Bobbie James'

R. gallica 'Versicolor'

'Bobbie James'

'Königin von Dänemark'

'Königin von Dänemark'

urn

'Maiden's Blush'

urn

'Madame Isaac Pereire'

'Noisette Carnée'

lawn

'Noisette Carnée'

'Duchesse d'Angoulême'

'Robert le Diable'

'Tuscany Superb'

'Ispahan'

'Madame Alfred Carrière'

'Madame Alfred Carrière'

'Duchesse d'Angoulême'

'Boule de Neige'

'Madame Hardy'

La Ville de Bruxelles'

SHOPPING LIST

HERBACEOUS PLANTING FOR THE POOL AREA

(see page 88 for suggestions for underplanting of the main rose beds)

9 *Iris* Blue Surprise
6 *Iris ensata* (syn. *I. kaempferi*), Deep Purple
10 *Viola cornuta*
12 *Viola odorata*

ROSES

2 'Alba Maxima'
8 'Alexandre Girault'
3 'Blanche Double de Coubert'
2 'Bobbie James'
1 'Boule de Neige'
1 *R. x centifolia* 'Shailer's White Moss'
10 'City of York' (syn. 'Direktör Benschop')
2 'Climbing Cécile Brünner'
10 'Climbing Iceberg'
2 'Comte de Chambord' (syn. 'Madame Knorr')
2 'Duchesse d'Angoulême'
4 'Fru Dagmar Hastrup'
1 *R. gallica* 'Versicolor'
1 'Ispahan'
2 'Janet B. Wood'
4 'Königin von Dänemark'
1 'La Ville de Bruxelles'
1 'Madame Hardy'
1 'Maiden's Blush'
2 'Madame Alfred Carrière'
3 'Madame Isaac Pereire'
2 'Noisette Carnée'
1 'Robert le Diable'
6 *R. x centifolia* 'De Meaux'
1 'Rose du Roi'
6 'Roseraie de l'Haÿ'
4 'Sarah van Fleet'
1 'Tuscany Superb'

SHRUBS

300 *Buxus sempervirens* (box) edging
15 *Lavandula* Giant White

Above, top: *Viola cornuta*
Above: *Iris ensata* Deep Purple
Opposite:
Top left: *Rosa* 'Roseraie de l'Haÿ'
Top centre: *Rosa* 'Noisette Carnée'
Top right: *Rosa* 'Madame Isaac Pereire'
Centre left: *Rosa* 'Blanche Double de Coubert'
Centre: *Rosa* 'Fru Dagmar Hastrup'
Centre right: *Rosa* 'Tuscany Superb'
Below left: *Rosa* 'Königin von Dänemark'
Below centre: *Rosa gallica* 'Versicolor'
Below right: *Rosa* 'Madame Hardy'

A DESERT GARDEN

THE GARDENS OF FRANK LLOYD WRIGHT IN
THE SOUTH-WESTERN USA

WHEN, IN THE 1920S AND '30S, the brilliant American architect Frank Lloyd Wright began to design buildings for the deserts and semi-deserts of Arizona and California, he became fascinated by ways of integrating his buildings into their extraordinary landscapes. Desert plants, too, intrigued him, for their adaptation to the extreme conditions often gave them remarkable shapes. Looking at the plants as architecture, Wright found worlds of triangles amongst the cactuses, both in the cross-sections of their trunks, and the intersections of their spines. Desert shrubs fascinated him too. Indeed the ocotillo (*Fouquieria splendens*), with its bunches of awkward stems and surprising plumes of coral-red flowers, became one of his favourite plants. In the wonderfully atmospheric drawings he prepared for clients, he often shows the local flora surrounding his buildings, and sweeping inwards, populating terraces and patios, dissolving the boundaries of the built and the natural.

The intense light was filled with possibility too. He rethought the bland concrete blocks commonly used for local buildings and they became, under his eye, magnificent abstract reliefs, whose repetition over whole façades gave many of his buildings sumptuous appeal. He wrote:

Aesthetically concrete has neither song nor any story. Nor is it easy to see in this conglomerate, in this mud pie, a high aesthetic property . . . [nevertheless] concrete is a plastic material – susceptible to the impress of imagination. I saw a kind of weaving coming out of it . . . Lightness and strength! Steel the spider spinning a web within the cheap, molded material and wedded to it by pouring an inner core of cement after the blocks were set up.

Many of his clients were wealthy. Their houses, which he set magnificently in the surrounding landscape, often had remarkable views. He was acutely aware of pre-Columbian American architecture, as well as the highly formal garden layouts of the ancient Middle East, and many of

Frank Lloyd Wright wrote, 'Architecture is the triumph of Human Imagination . . . It is at least the geometric pattern of things, of life, of the human and social world.' Here at La Miniatura, the Alice Millard House in Pasadena, the arching forms of the planting envelop and frame the house, providing a graceful counterpoint to the rectangular blocks and geometric decoration of the architecture, while the golden Californian light brings vivid life to the building and its plantings.

Above: Frank Lloyd Wright's romantic but botanically schematic drawings give a picture of the sort of plantings he imagined for his marvellous buildings. Here, he originally envisaged strongly vertical lines of planting to contrast with the craggy horizontals of concrete. A proposed pool reflects both.

Opposite: The light and shadow from the garden trees give life to the richly textured walls; a simple planting combination of neat horizontal groundcover and the vertical trees sets off the complex, decorative block patterns.

his proposals had a quite epic scale. By the time he was designing desert houses in the 1930s, Wright also knew European and Japanese enclosed gardens well, and used some of their elements close to his buildings or as part of their internal spaces.

NOTES ON THE PLAN

The plan, notably in its built elements, makes use of some of the features that he gave the garden of La Miniatura, the house he designed in 1923 for Alice Millard. This was the first of the 'textile-block' houses he built for clients in California; and the desert house he later built for himself over the border in Arizona is in the same idiom. The plan, following Wright's preferences, also uses plants native to the desert states of North America, and a few from Mexico. It assumes, though, that the garden has no extensive view outwards, and so makes the design a series of linked inward-looking spaces, each different in character. It contains variations in level, with walled raised beds, to give a sense of dynamic 'landscape', though these would be easily altered to suit the site. The treatment of the site's boundary is not specified. Similarly decorated walls would be ideal, but may not be possible in your locality. If you prefer a hedged boundary, tightly clipped *Thuja plicata* would work in suitable areas, but ocotillo, or even organ pipe cactus, can be used in drier conditions.

BUILDING IT

The most important element of the look resides in the internal walls. Wright developed the standard concrete building block into what he called 'textile blocks', where humble concrete was cast into complex and elegant patterns. He used various sizes, but eventually the most common was 40 x 40 x 9cm/ 16 x 16 x 3½in. All had to be hand-cast. The depth of the relief was often around 7cm/3in, though some blocks were pierced right through. Later designs are exceptionally complex, but in a small space simplifications will work just as well. Wright often used two or more patterns of block for each scheme,

using half- or third-width blocks for corners, copings and so on. It is best if you discuss your needs with a local concrete specialist. If necessary, build a maquette from superimposed layers of plywood or board, and get the concrete specialist to cast as many copies as you need. In many textile-block houses, the blocks are knitted together with steel rods, the gap between them and the interior skin of the house being left as cavity air space for insulation. If you are not a materials purist, get the maquette copied in fibreglass or plastic, and apply the panels to a basic concrete wall.

The 2.5m/8ft-high screen walls only need a single band of decorative blocks one block width below the top of the wall. The screen wall backing the pool would look good with several contiguous rows. Score the render on the rest of the wall with a grid of lines to suggest the use of blank blocks; Wright loved juxtaposing blank surfaces with gorgeously patterned ones. The two low retaining walls give relief to the central planting; use patterned blocks here.

The terrace paving, the broad step down to the pool garden and the main pathways through the garden are made from units with the same dimensions as the blocks. If these are being cast too, give them a small groove 6mm/¼in deep and across, 2.5cm/1in inside the block's margin, to emphasize the design.

You can use a commercial fibreglass pool, or a specialist can easily make one up to suit the space available. Here, it is raised 40cm/16in above ground level, and rimmed with decorated blocks. Immediately backed by the screen wall, the pool is fed by a simple brass spigot, attached either to a recycling pump or to the house's water supply. The only parts of the planting needing irrigation are the area of grass around the pools, and the big pots on the terrace.

For a dawn coffee or a moonlight drink, the seats are placed with views of the garden. A simple plinth of concrete is enough, softened with cushions when in use. For when the sun is higher, the pergola area can be planted for shade with vines or even, in warm regions, with scrambling cacti like *Selenicereus* or *Hylocactus*, both night-flowering and heavily perfumed. Support the pergola either on piers of timber or on decorative blocks.

PLANTING AND MAINTAINING IT

If you want to bring on the design quickly, you can use semi-mature plants for the peripheral planting, especially behind the screen wall. Some of the cacti, and certainly the ocotillos, will need to be ordered from specialist suppliers. Try to make sure that they are of cultivated material, not plants rustled from the wild. Most will tolerate some cold, but if your area drops much below 4C/40°F, grow them in easily lifted pots, and store indoors over winter. The ephemeral annuals will mostly seed vigorously; thin seedlings to stop them swamping the lower-growing perennials and valuable cacti. Use them to create drifts of colour, from the intense blues of the phacelias and the smokier ones of the lupins, to the pale shades of oenothera and stocks. They'll soon give way to the rich colours of perennials like the penstemons, the plummy red sphaeralceas, and the wonderfully perfumed violet mirabilis. The regional cacti, especially the *Echinocereus* species, can produce some spectacular flowers. *Peniocerus greggii* should be grown for its astonishing smell.

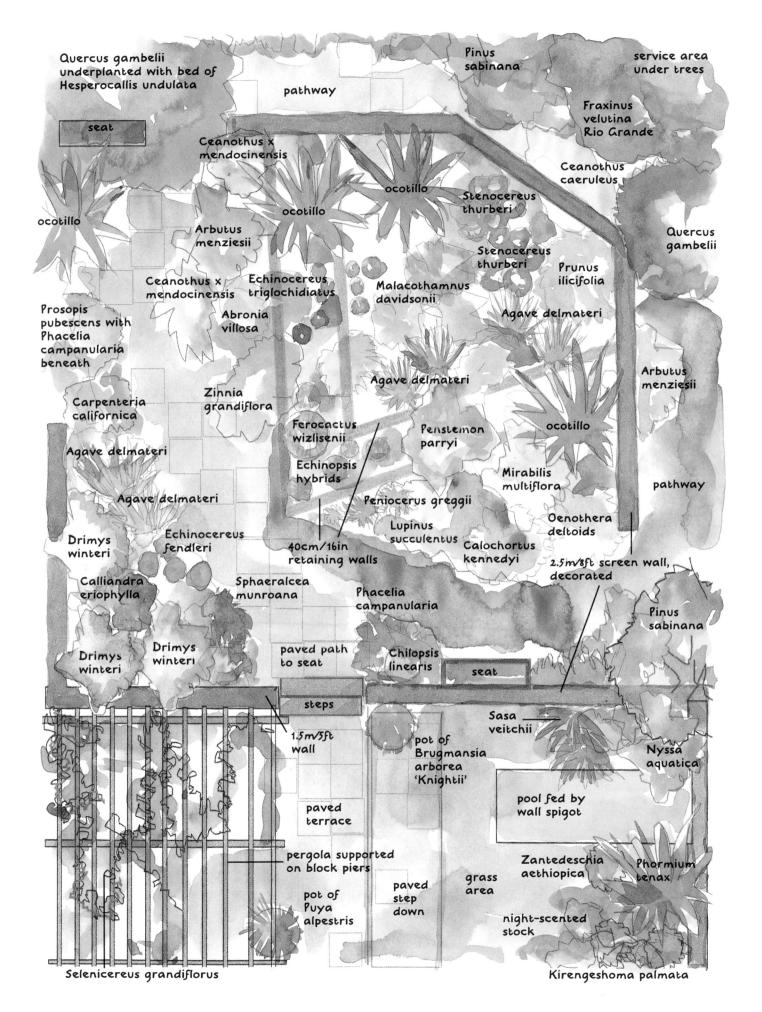

Quercus gambelii
underplanted with bed of
Hesperocallis undulata

pathway

Pinus
sabinana

service area
under trees

seat

Ceanothus x
mendocinensis

ocotillo

ocotillo

Stenocereus
thurberi

Fraxinus
velutina
Rio Grande

Ceanothus
caeruleus

ocotillo

ocotillo

Arbutus
menziesii

Ceanothus x
mendocinensis

Echinocereus
triglochidiatus

Malacothamnus
davidsonii

Stenocereus
thurberi

Prunus
ilicifolia

Quercus
gambelii

Prosopis
pubescens with
Phacelia
campanularia
beneath

Abronia
villosa

Agave delmateri

Agave delmateri

Arbutus
menziesii

Carpenteria
californica

Zinnia
grandiflora

Agave delmateri

Ferocactus
wizlisenii

Penstemon
parryi

ocotillo

Agave delmateri

Echinopsis
hybrids

Mirabilis
multiflora

pathway

Agave delmateri

Peniocereus greggii

Drimys
winteri

Echinocereus
fendleri

Lupinus
succulentus

Oenothera
deltoids

Calliandra
eriophylla

Sphaeralcea
munroana

40cm/16in
retaining walls

Calochortus
kennedyi

2.5m/8ft screen wall,
decorated

Phacelia
campanularia

Pinus
sabinana

Drimys
winteri

Drimys
winteri

paved path
to seat

Chilopsis
linearis

seat

Nyssa
aquatica

steps

Sasa
veitchii

1.5m/5ft
wall

pot of
Brugmansia
arborea
'Knightii'

paved
terrace

pool fed by
wall spigot

pergola supported
on block piers

Zantedeschia
aethiopica

Phormium
tenax

pot of
Puya
alpestris

paved
step
down

grass
area

night-scented
stock

Selenicereus grandiflorus

Kirengeshoma palmata

SHOPPING LIST

ANNUALS AND BIENNIALS

25 *Abronia villosa*

40 *Lupinus succulentus*

25 *Oenothera deltoides*

40 *Phacelia campanularia*

15 *Zinnia grandiflora*

BULBS

40 *Calochortus kennedyi*

40 *Hesperocallis undulata*

BUSH

1 *Prunus ilicifolia*

CACTUSES

8 *Echinocereus triglochidiatus*

5 *Echinocereus fendleri*

5 *Echinopsis* hybrids

5 *Ferocactus wizliseni*

3 *Peniocerus greggii*

2 *Stenocereus thurberi*

HERBACEOUS PLANTING

25 *Mirabilis multiflora*

15 *Penstemon parryi*

SCRAMBLER

1 *Selenicereus grandiflorus*

SHRUBS

6 *Agave delmateri*

1 *Calliandra eriophylla*

1 *Carpenteria californica*

1 *Ceanothus caeruleus*

3 *Ceanothus x mendocinensis*

1 *Chilopsis linearis*

3 *Drimys winteri*

4 *Fouquieria splendens* (ocotillo)

7 *Malacothamnus* (Sphaeralcea) *davidsonii*

3 *Sphaeralcea munroana*

TREES

2 *Arbutus menziesii*

1 *Fraxinus velutina* Rio Grande

1 *Pinus sabinana*

1 *Prosopis pubescens*

2 *Quercus gambelii*

POOL GARDEN

3 *Brugmansia arborea* 'Knightii'

3 *Kirengeshoma palmata*

1 pkt *Matthiola bicornis* (night-scented stock)

1 *Nyssa aquatica*

1 *Phormium tenax*

3 *Puya alpestris*

3 *Sasa veitchii*

6 *Zantedeschia aethiopica*

Above: *Brugmansia arborea* 'Knightii'
Opposite top left: *Echinopsis* hybrid
Opposite top centre: *Drimys winteri*
Opposite top right: *Penstemon parryi*
Opposite below left: *Phormium tenax*
Opposite centre right: *Fouquieria splendens*
Opposite bottom right: *Carpenteria californica*

A TOPIARY ROOM
LAWRENCE JOHNSTON AT HIDCOTE MANOR

T OPIARY IS SPECIAL. Sitting in a topiary garden, even a half-ruined one, with weedy paths and orange pumpkins sitting where there should have been flowers, is a magical experience. As the sun sets, the great columns and obelisks of yew and box become shadowy blue, and have their own still presence. This topiary garden is at Hidcote Manor, with its four now heavily stylized peacocks, and was just as magical. It was built as part of a dream. The estate was bought by a wealthy, and domineering, Anglo-American woman and her Paris-born son. She seems not to have been mightily interested in dreams, but her son, Lawrence Johnston (1871–1958), suffering intense Anglophilia, wanted to become a Cotswold gentleman. He had the means, he had the house. He needed the garden, however, for the house as yet had nothing but a few ancient cedar trees. The new garden, which was to become so beautiful, started off shakily from a dull and conventional start. Then his 'eye' developed. The garden became an obsession – at least the planning, and the collection of its plants, did.

The garden developed first as a series of enclosed spaces, leading on to splendid vistas, some copying, and others developing, ideas of the 17th-century French gardens. Pools, a grass theatre and lavish flower beds were soon added. This lovely topiary garden started out with tiny box edges, and skinny peacocks atop their poles. It now has thick chunky hedges, and the peacocks have fattened up vastly to sit, heavily anchored and full of character, on their bases.

Of course, topiary takes time. Box, well looked after, can put on 15–20cm/6–8in of growth in a season. But it needs cutting back in order to make it branch, and so thicken up. A hedge, say 45cm/18in high, and as much deep, will take six or seven seasons to create. Add another couple of seasons at least for the decorative flourishes. Topiary is the absolute antithesis to anything instant. But though instant gardening may seem magical at the time, the magic evaporates in a fortnight at most, while this magic grows and grows, and will hold you in its spell all year long, and for year upon year.

Lawrence Johnston had staff to shear and clear the clippings. In fact, the modern machinery makes topiary easy. You would need two weekends a season to keep a topiary garden like this mostly in shape, and perhaps an extra weekend for the backing hedges.

At Hidcote, the solid walls of yew, the hedges, and the dumpy and now rather 'cubist' topiary peacocks of box make a strong frame for generous plantings. Here, they are mostly in pale tones. The dark background makes all colours glow with life.

NOTES ON THE PLAN

The topiary garden at Hidcote has had various plantings through its lifetime. Now, it's a white garden. It is possible to transpose the plantings on pages 113–115 to these beds if you want this sort of white garden, but the plan here is inspired by Hidcote's famous red borders. These vary in their composition from season to season, and the plan (as the garden did in Johnston's day) departs from the strictly red. In any case, an all-red scene needs some contrast. The plan adds the silvery grey filigree of *Artemisia* 'Powis Castle', and the sultry purple-blue of *Salvia* x *superba*, a fine plant in which the flowers are intensely blue, and the inflated sepals and bracts are rosy purple. For more contrast still, the tubs by the benches are planted with the creamy-white-flowered *Hydrangea paniculata* 'Grandiflora', at Hidcote grown in the Old Garden beneath the cedars.

Right: In the famous red borders at Hidcote, the warm shades shine like jewels; the planting, designed to make the blue distance look even more remote, has been adapted in the plan here to fit into the enclosed green framework of the white topiary garden.

Below: The topiary birds, now more pouting pigeon than peacock, sit on box drums; topiary enthusiasts might ensure that drum, bird and surrounding hedges were made of different varieties of box, which would be best, or even of different plants. Beasts and supports like these might take seven to ten years to build, but are immensely rewarding thereafter.

BUILDING IT

The pale biscuit-coloured sand from the lower part of the Loire valley is the ideal material for the paths. If you don't have access to this, or something similar, then a brown or a neutral-grey brick, laid in a herringbone pattern, would be excellent. If you are not adept at cutting bricks, leave the edge of the path zig-zagged and let the box edging hide the raggedness.

The plan suggests classical stone benches; these are good on a summer day, cold or even damp on any other, and need cushions on all. Wood is friendlier, if less architectural, and can be painted. A slatey blue-grey would be good. White is not an option.

The tubs in the plan can easily be half-barrels, as once in the Cottage Garden at Hidcote. They give a pleasantly rustic feel to the view. Versailles tubs would be grander, and much more expensive.

PLANTING AND MAINTAINING IT

The hedging and box edging are treated in the standard way. Forming the topiary detail is also easy. Some gardeners build a stout wire framework that outlines the final desired form of the future topiary. Plant stems are trained into it, then clipped as they exceed its boundaries. Others let the plants grow into a loose bush, of approximately the right size, then begin to form the desired shape from that. Secateurs are good for this sort of work.

During the various heydays of topiary, in late-Renaissance gardens, and then again in the mid- and late 19th century, it was common to find the decorative detail in a scheme like this carried out in a different plant. A golden yew globe on a box hedge, or a holly obelisk on a yew one.

The backing hedging at Hidcote is of yew. It is possible to buy semi-mature yew plants 1m/3½ft or more high, though it would still take the plants five seasons or so to make a unified hedge 2m/6½ft high. Young plants less than 30cm/1ft high, if well fed, can put on between 15cm/6in and 30cm/1ft a season, with the average being at the lower end of those figures. Plant 45cm/18in–60cm/2ft apart. Plants will develop a 'leader' shoot. Take the tip off this as it develops to encourage side branching.

It would be possible to use faster-growing species – privet, holly, *Lonicera nitida*, even some of the faster-growing conifer species – but nothing gives the velvety darkness of yew. Holly is good, though the clippings are hard to handle. The conifer generally called leylandii is by far the least satisfactory, with a depressing texture and often going bald at the base.

Otherwise, the flower garden is maintained in a standard manner. The acanthus, once established, will produce runners. Either dig them up, or spray with a systemic weedkiller, which seems not to spread back to the main plant. *Salvia sclarea* var. *turkestaniana* is a biennial. With its huge cloudy blue-grey bracts and hooked white flowers, it is so worth having that you probably won't mind looking after a sequence of seedlings. *Salvia microphylla* will not survive hard frosts. Lift, and overwinter away from the cold. Cuttings root easily if you need them. The dahlias should be lifted too, though they will survive a mild winter. The penstemons – here the purplish 'Garnet' (syn. 'Andenken an Friedrich Hahn'), though there are many proper scarlets if you prefer – are also not hardy in cold northern gardens. Again, lift a few plants and overwinter somewhere frost free. In the spring, new growth is easily rooted. The kniphofia 'Lord Roberts', tall and stately, is a thrilling salmony red. If it's not to be found, any tall good red (such as 'John Benary', which is, or is almost, identical) will do.

The tubs need little help apart from regular watering and feeding. Vine weevil grubs like hydrangea roots and can eat them completely so that the plant blows away. Keep watch for adults. The grubs can be attacked with parasites that are watered in, or with chemicals. Healthy plants will still be in flower in November. For the pots on the terrace, the choice is up to you. *Narcissus* 'Thalia' would be pretty in spring; for summer, try a good Hidcote planting – the old zonal pelargonium, rusty red-flowered, called 'Burton's Variety', *Helichrysum petiolare* 'Limelight' and a few plants of red-leaved *Atriplex*.

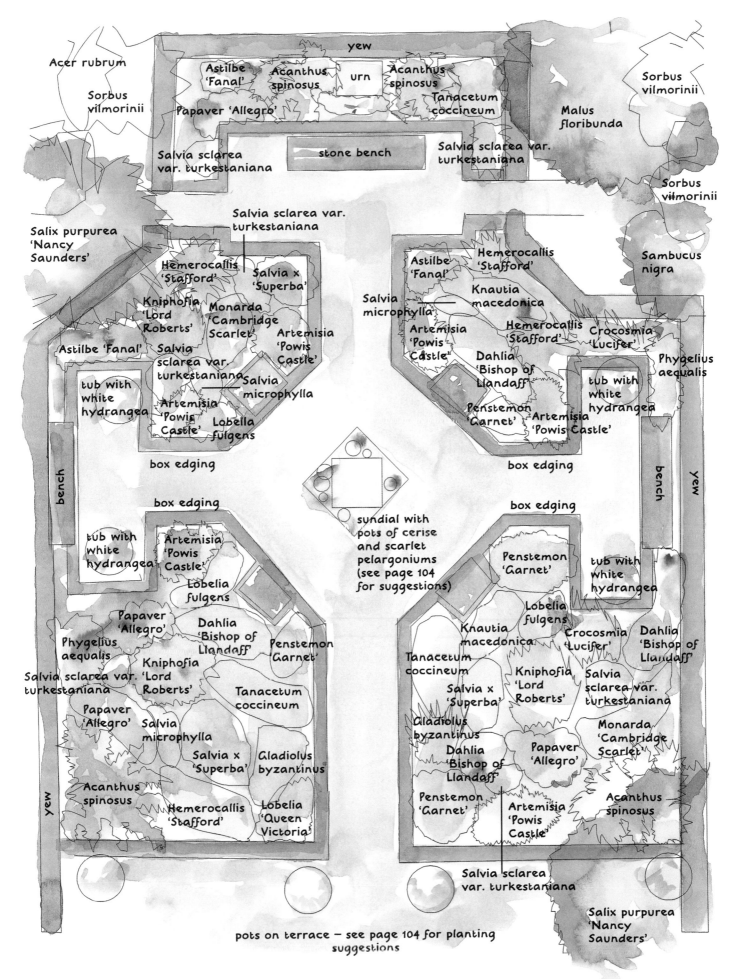

Acer rubrum

Sorbus
vilmorinii

yew

Astilbe
'Fanal'

Acanthus
spinosus

urn

Acanthus
spinosus

Tanacetum
coccineum

Sorbus
vilmorinii

Malus
floribunda

Papaver 'Allegro'

Salvia sclarea
var. turkestaniana

stone bench

Salvia sclarea var.
turkestaniana

Sorbus
vilmorinii

Salix purpurea
'Nancy
Saunders'

Salvia sclarea var.
turkestaniana

Hemerocallis
'Stafford'

Salvia x
'Superba'

Astilbe
'Fanal'

Hemerocallis
'Stafford'

Sambucus
nigra

Kniphofia
'Lord
Roberts'

Monarda
'Cambridge
Scarlet'

Artemisia
'Powis
Castle'

Salvia
microphylla

Knautia
macedonica

Astilbe 'Fanal'

Salvia
sclarea var.
turkestaniana

Salvia
microphylla

Artemisia
'Powis
Castle'

Hemerocallis
'Stafford'

Crocosmia
'Lucifer'

tub with
white
hydrangea

Artemisia
'Powis
Castle'

Lobelia
fulgens

Dahlia
'Bishop of
Llandaff'

Penstemon
'Garnet'

tub with
white
hydrangea

Phygelius
aequalis

Artemisia
'Powis Castle'

box edging

box edging

box edging

bench

yew

box edging

tub with
white
hydrangea

Artemisia
'Powis
Castle'

sundial with
pots of cerise
and scarlet
pelargoniums
(see page 104
for suggestions)

Penstemon
'Garnet'

tub with
white
hydrangea

bench

Lobelia
fulgens

Lobelia
fulgens

Papaver
'Allegro'

Dahlia
'Bishop of
Llandaff'

Penstemon
'Garnet'

Knautia
macedonica

Crocosmia
'Lucifer'

Dahlia
'Bishop of
Llandaff'

Phygelius
aequalis

Kniphofia
'Lord
Roberts'

Tanacetum
coccineum

Tanacetum
coccineum

Salvia x
'Superba'

Kniphofia
'Lord
Roberts'

Salvia
sclarea var.
turkestaniana

Salvia sclarea var.
turkestaniana

Papaver
'Allegro'

Salvia
microphylla

Gladiolus
byzantinus

Monarda
'Cambridge
Scarlet'

Salvia x
'Superba'

Gladiolus
byzantinus

Dahlia
'Bishop of
Llandaff'

Papaver
'Allegro'

Acanthus
spinosus

Hemerocallis
'Stafford'

Lobelia
'Queen
Victoria'

Penstemon
'Garnet'

Artemisia
'Powis
Castle'

Acanthus
spinosus

yew

Salvia sclarea
var. turkestaniana

Salix purpurea
'Nancy
Saunders'

pots on terrace — see page 104 for planting
suggestions

SHOPPING LIST

BULBS

100 *Gladiolus communis* subsp. *byzantinus*

HEDGING

400 *Buxus sempervirens* (box)

350 *Taxus baccata* (yew)

HERBACEOUS PLANTING

4 *Acanthus spinosus*

6 *Artemisia* 'Powis Castle'

9 *Astilbe* x *arendsii* 'Fanal'

6 *Crocosmia* 'Lucifer'

12 *Dahlia* 'Bishop of Llandaff'

12 *Hemerocallis* 'Stafford'

6 *Knautia macedonica*

9 *Kniphofia* 'Lord Roberts'

6 *Lobelia fulgens*

6 *Lobelia* 'Queen Victoria'

9 *Monarda* 'Cambridge Scarlet'

9 *Papaver orientale* 'Allegro'

18 *Penstemon* 'Garnet' (syn. 'Andenken an Friedrich Hahn')

4 *Salvia microphylla*

9 *Salvia* x 'Superba'

12 *Tanacetum coccineum*

SEED

21 plants a season *Salvia sclarea* var. *turkestaniana*

SHRUBS

4 *Hydrangea paniculata* 'Grandiflora' (white hydrangea)

2 *Phygelius aequalis*

TREES

1 *Acer rubrum*

1 *Malus floribunda*

2 *Salix purpurea* 'Nancy Saunders'

1 *Sambucus nigra*

3 *Sorbus vilmorinii*

Right top: *Papaver orientale* 'Allegro'
Right below: *Monarda* 'Cambridge Scarlet'
Opposite top left: *Kniphofia* 'Lord Roberts'
Opposite top centre: *Hemerocallis* 'Stafford'
Opposite top right: *Knautia macedonica*
Opposite bottom left: *Dahlia* 'Bishop of Llandaff'
Opposite bottom right: *Acanthus spinosus*

THE ENGLISH GARDEN DREAM

VITA SACKVILLE-WEST'S WHITE GARDEN
AT SISSINGHURST CASTLE

THE WHITE GARDEN at Sissinghurst Castle is one of the most widely admired designs in Britain. It was created by the novelist and poet Vita Sackville-West, and while her novels and poems are now almost forgotten, her marvellous plantings around the castle and its medieval moat still thrill visitors, who come away enthralled and envious. The story is an extraordinary one. Vita Sackville-West (1892–1962) was born in the Sackvilles' immense, and immensely romantic, medieval house of Knole, given by Queen Elizabeth I to her cousin Thomas Sackville in 1566. However, Vita, though an only child, was prevented by her sex from inheriting the estate. Its loss fuelled her imagination, and a need to re-create something in its place. After her marriage in 1913, she created a pleasant but ordinary garden at a Kentish house called Long Barn, before she stumbled upon the site of her dreams while house-hunting in early 1930.

What swept her off her feet were half-ruined fragments of another great house – Sissinghurst Castle. The glorious Elizabethan gatehouse tower, some service quarters and part of the medieval moat were all that were left. Nevertheless, even the remains were impossibly romantic. She shook her rickety finances together and bought the place. It set her imagination free.

She and her husband at once started planning a garden, in which she wanted a glorious abundance of flowers, and he a rational and formal layout. Although she was by now a well-known and well-regarded writer, the force of her energy and intellect became most intensely engaged by her unconventional house and its grounds. She began to write about gardens and gardening in the 1930s, and her books, her series of gardening articles for the *Observer* and her epic poem *The Garden* (1946) have, with the garden, ensured her fame.

Vita planted bounteously: plants that were beautiful, plants that had romantic stories; almost everything she did looked wonderful. The most famous part of her garden, the white garden, though not the first of its kind, struck and still strikes a chord with all sorts of gardener, and is one of the great classics of its time. She used white of all hues, from the ivory or blush whites of roses to the translucent whites of mallows, the white-

One of the reasons that many of the white plantings at Sissinghurst Castle are so satisfying is that they are built up with interesting foliage as well as with flowers, and that both can vary from exquisite delicacy to extreme boldness. Here, the jagged silvery foliage of the giant eryngium Miss Willmott's ghost counterpoints the white lupin's stiff spires and the soft round forms of the roses.

Left: As the garden at Sissinghurst showed, white can be as powerfully expressive in the garden as any other colour; here, white phlox and roses are all of a translucent and ephemeral delicacy, whereas the calla lilies manage to be both erotic and icy at the same time.

Right: The extraordinary and exuberant canopy of Rosa mulliganii *covers the gothic arbour in the White Garden in early summer; the vase sits in the shadows, mysterious and serene.*

felted foliage of artemisias, and the grey-greens of eryngiums and the silver pear trees. Admiration of her white garden became a badge of the educated gardener.

NOTES ON THE PLAN

The plan combines two elements of Sissinghurst: the dining area near the cottage, and the famous white garden, here with the circular pergola cut in half and moved to the far end of the space, and covered with the rose from the gable wall of the cottage – 'Madame Alfred Carrière'. She can flower from late spring, and still have a scattering of buds until the first hard frosts.

All the gardens at Sissinghurst are enclosed by hedges or walls, making each section autonomous. Here, the plan assumes enclosure, but if your garden has none, double the depth of the enclosing plantings,

though the rose obelisks (or tall pyramids of poles) should be left as singles.

The plan gives no planting for early spring bulbs, but the season will start in March with pulmonarias and anemones. Add white narcissus, hyacinths or muscaris, or use the shopping list for bulbs on page 38. Leave them in the ground from season to season, and divide and replant at the same time as the herbaceous planting.

BUILDING IT

A gravel and sand mix is fine for paths, though, as the point of a white garden is to look at subtleties of colour and form, brick or stone paving is better still. Setts would be best of all, especially the dark neutral-grey sort used for late-19th-century roadways. If obtainable, these can be set in a sand and concrete mix.

The rose pyramids that give height and form to the centre of the four parterre beds, and along the side plantings, are easily built from four poles about 3m/10ft long. Often called 'stobs', if pressure-treated with preservatives they will last a dozen years at least. Ensure that the preservative is clear, not coloured. Sink 60cm/2ft or so of each pole into the soil, slanted so that the tops of the poles can be nailed or tied together. Plant the rose to one side, and tie in shoots, wound spirally, as they grow.

The semicircular pergola or gazebo could be built with solid rods, as at Sissinghurst, or with iron piping from a plumbers' yard. The roof should be domed, both for the look of the thing, and also to make it stronger – even iron piping, horizontal, would sag beneath the weight of the rose. The structure should also be well anchored. The sheet of vegetation it supports can act like a sail in a high wind and uproot the whole thing. The rose needs to be tied in securely. Trying to get half a ton of windblown rose back on its perch is a major and unpleasant undertaking. Aluminium piping, of the sort used to build polytunnels, is not strong enough for the job.

Otherwise, this is a plantsperson's garden, though the quality of the pots for the terrace and the gazebo is important. Fill Ali Baba jars with malvas and malvastrum, and big earthenware pots with *Verbena* 'Sissinghurst', *Sphaeralcea munroana* and, for summer, tobacco (*Nicotiana sylvestris*) or white lilies, white narcissus or hyacinths for spring. New pots need ageing. Give them a wash of mud, milk and a teaspoon of fertilizer to encourage the swift growth of moss and lichen. Alternatively, sponge on very dilute white emulsion paint.

PLANTING AND MAINTAINING IT

Scale is given to the garden by the silver pear trees (*Pyrus salicifolia* 'Pendula'). These are usually grafted on to a tall stock of another sort of pear. Silver pear is vigorous and fast-growing and will look charming for the first five or six seasons. Trim any pendulous stems that get in the way. By its seventh season, the head of the tree will have become a dark dense tangle. As all branches happily produce side branches along their length, and these insist on growing at 90 degrees to the parental branch, trying to thin the heads out is a frustrating and time-consuming business. Be tough and cut out whole sections, freeing them from the rest of the tangle with a chain saw; by summer the trees will look fine again, and the plants beneath will have plenty of light once more.

Buying and planting the roses is easy. The shrub roses need thinning once they become too tangled. 'Madame Alfred Carrière', with long and not extensively branched stems, is easily thinned by cutting out whole branches at a time. Harsh winters can sometimes kill it to the ground. It soon regrows.

A number of the herbaceous plants are heavy-duty thugs, and will take over the garden if allowed. Watch particularly the white fireweed (*Epilobium*); its green rhizomes will snake through your beds strangling as they go. They don't run deep, so are fairly easily controlled. Double white soapwort is another thug, its thin roots cheerfully penetrating tarmac and old walls. It smells so good in flower, perhaps you won't mind. For maintenance of the herbaceous plants, see page 72.

The soft-coloured *Malva sylvestris* 'Primley Blue' will need spraying for rust fungus, as will *Malvastrum lateritium* in the pots. The malvastrum has curious apricot flowers with rose pink centres. *Verbena* 'Sissinghurst' is not hardy, and needs overwintering away from frost. Under cover, it gets greenfly badly, sometimes fatally. Watch and spray.

KEY TO PLANTS ON THE PLAN

A: *Anemone rivularis*
B: *Epilobium angustifolium* 'Album'
C: *Malva moschata* f. *alba*
D: *Alchemilla mollis*
E: *Lilium martagon* var. *album*
F: *Paradisea liliastrum*
G: *Artemisia* 'Powis Castle'
H: *Vinca minor* f. *alba*
I: *Papaver* 'Perry's White'
Rose 1: *Rosa* 'Madame Hardy'
Rose 2: *Rosa* 'Alba Maxima'
Rose 3: *Rosa* 'Madame Plantier'

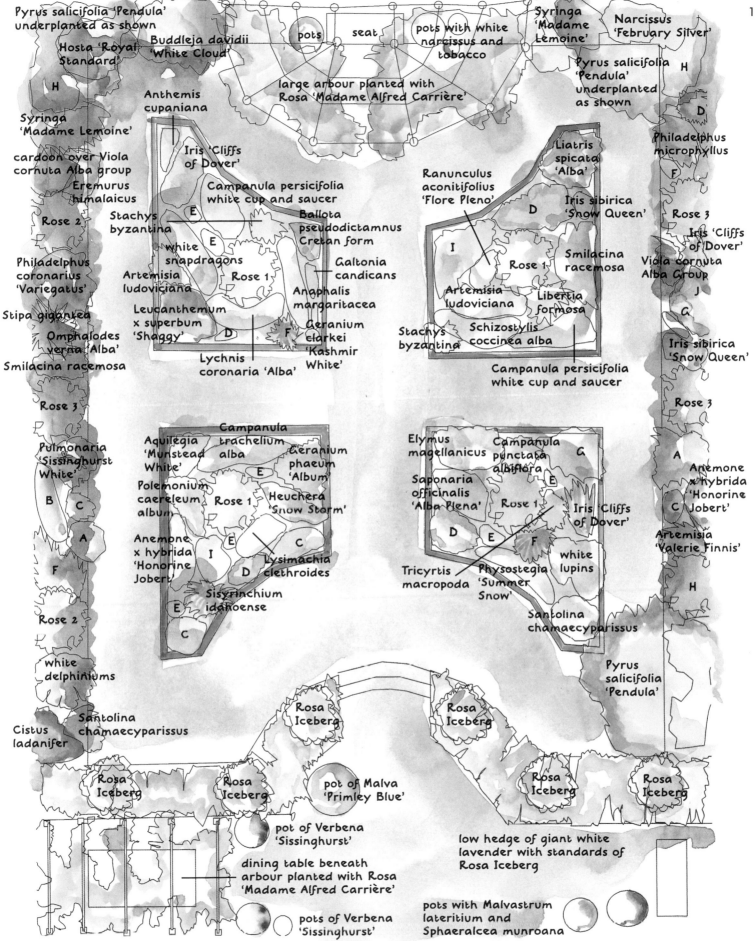

Above: *Rosa* 'Madame Alfred Carrière'
Below: *Epilobium angustifolium* 'Album'
Opposite left: *Nicotiana sylvestris*
Opposite top centre: *Aquilegia* 'Munstead White'
Opposite top right: *Schizostylis coccinea* f. *alba*
Opposite bottom right: *Artemisia ludoviciana* 'Valerie Finnis'

SHOPPING LIST

BULBS

6 *Eremurus himalaicus*

6 *Galtonia candicans*

12 *Lilium martagon* var. *album*

100 *Narcissus* 'February Silver'

SEED

Antirrhinum (snapdragons), white

Cynara cardunculus (cardoon)

Nicotiana sylvestris

HERBACEOUS PLANTING

12 *Alchemilla mollis*

3 *Anaphalis margaritacea*

3 *Anemone* x *hybrida* 'Honorine Jobert'

6 *Anemone rivularis*

1 *Anthemis punctata* subsp. *cupaniana*

3 *Aquilegia* 'Munstead White'

1 *Artemisia ludoviciana*

1 *Artemisia* 'Powis Castle'

6 *Artemisia ludoviciana* 'Valerie Finnis'

1 *Ballota pseudodictamnus* Cretan form

6 *Campanula persicifolia* white cup and saucer

1 *Campanula punctata* f. *albiflora*

6 *Campanula trachelium* var. *alba*

3 *Delphinium* white variety

3 *Elymus magellanicus* (syn. *Agropyron pubiflorum*)

6 *Epilobium angustifolium* 'Album'

3 *Geranium clarkei* 'Kashmir White'

3 *Geranium phaeum* 'Album'

5 *Heuchera sanguinea* 'Snowstorm'

6 *Hosta* 'Royal Standard'

6 *Iris* 'Cliffs of Dover'

6 *Iris sibirica* 'Snow Queen'

3 *Leucanthemum* x *superbum* 'Shaggy'

3 *Liatris spicata* 'Alba'

5 *Libertia formosa*

1 *Lupinus* white variety

2 *Lychnis coronaria* 'Alba'

3 *Lysimachia clethroides*

3 *Malva sylvestris* 'Primley Blue'

6 *Malva moschata* f. *alba*

3 *Malvastrum lateritium*

6 *Omphalodes verna* 'Alba'

2 *Papaver orientale* 'Perry's White'

12 *Paradisea liliastrum*

1 *Physostegia virginiana* 'Summer Snow'

6 *Polemonium caeruleum* f. *album*

12 *Pulmonaria* 'Sissinghurst White'

1 *Ranunculus aconitifolius* 'Flore Pleno'

2 *Santolina chamaecyparissus*

1 *Saponaria officinalis* 'Alba Plena'

3 *Schizostylis coccinea* f. *alba*

3 *Sisyrinchium idahoense*

2 *Smilacina racemosa*

3 *Sphaeralcea munroana*

3 *Stachys byzantina*

1 *Stipa gigantea*

3 *Tricyrtis macropoda*

9 *Verbena* 'Sissinghurst'

15 *Vinca minor* f. *alba*

12 *Viola cornuta* Alba Group

ROSES

4 *Rosa* 'Madame Hardy'

3 *Rosa* x *alba* 'Alba Maxima'

3 *Rosa* 'Madame Plantier'

6 *Rosa* Iceberg

6 *Rosa* 'Madame Alfred Carrière'

SHRUBS AND TREES

1 *Buddleja davidii* 'White Cloud'

1 *Cistus ladanifer*

30 *Lavandula* Giant White

1 *Philadelphus coronarius* 'Variegatus'

3 *Philadelphus microphyllus*

2 *Syringa vulgaris* 'Madame Lemoine' (lilac)

3 *Pyrus salicifolia* 'Pendula'

THE QUINTESSENTIAL COTTAGE GARDEN

MARGERY FISH AT EAST LAMBROOK MANOR

The 'crazy paving' paths made of field- and flagstone make a delightful and informal foil to the overflowing mass of hydrangeas, roses, Alchemilla mollis and other herbaceous planting. Seedlings abound in path and border, and clematis is allowed to scramble through the luxuriant vegetation.

THE ROMANTIC VIEW OF THE COTTAGE GARDEN was one of the consequences of the Industrial Revolution, when city-dwellers, at least the prosperous ones, remembered with affection the life that their parents or grandparents had seemed to live in the country. The 'cottage garden' came to represent a golden age of simplicity, harmony and rustic delight, when roses, honeysuckle and clematis garlanded the door, the storehouse or attic was filled with apples and pumpkins, and chickens scratched cheerfully through the flower-filled borders of summer.

New garden flowers began to appear in huge numbers in the late 19th century, so much so that a counter-movement began, and some gardeners started to collect old-fashioned garden plants instead, some of which had been widely grown since the late 16th century, and were in danger of disappearing. Old pinks, old auriculas, the rose plantain, old wallflowers and dozens more were rescued from out-of-the-way gardens and still delight us today.

The movement survived the Second World War, when Margery Fish (1888–1969) began to write about the garden she was creating around a golden and rustic manor house in East Lambrook in Somerset. Though she liked all sorts of plants (except the brilliant dahlias so loved by her late husband) she had a special affection for garden antiques collected from local village gardens. One favourite was the lovely and now well known old pink 'Brympton Red': apparently, at some unspecified date, Lady Lilian Digby found a nice pink in the workhouse garden at Beaminster in Dorset, and put cuttings in the garden at Brympton d'Evercy near Sherborne; Margery Fish, friendly with later owners of that handsome house, gave it the name and brought it into commerce at her nursery.

Her many books created an interest both in her style of gardening and in her garden. Both were immensely popular by the middle of the 20th century, partly because she wrote in a simpler and more straightforward way than the fanciful, stylish and more erudite Vita Sackville-West. Many readers would also have identified more easily with her relatively modest lifestyle, even with her penchant for shapeless frocks, than they could with louche Elizabethan Vita dressed in corduroy breeches and riding boots.

The crucial thing, though, is that Mrs Fish had an exceptional eye for a good plant, and almost anything grown by her is worth having in the garden.

She was an especially avid collector of plants, and concentrated on particular groups of species within various genera – for instance, the larger euphorbias, the silver-leaved artemisias, polyanthus primulas, 'pinks' amongst *Dianthus* and so on. Because of this, her garden produced remarkable numbers of pretty hybrids. Any plant with her or her demesne's name attached is something to grow in quantity.

BUILDING IT

This plan is primarily a plantsperson's garden. The emphasis is on fine plants and planting, and so there is little building work needed to re-create it.

The path is made of crazy paving, which can look as ugly as the phrase. Use stone fragments, even field-stone, rather than irregular chunks of concrete paving. If you choose field-stone, which comes in unequal sizes, there's no point in using landscape netting to any degree. Just bed the stones into the soil, with the flattest surface on top; if the stones are 20–30cm/ 8–12in or more across, and are bedded with care, they will remain perfectly stable, and there will be no need to concrete them in place. Weedkill now and again, or even moss-kill if the stone is a sandstone and it gets slippery. The path needs to be a yard across, and could be built right around the lawn. However, Mrs Fish didn't in the least mind her herbaceous plants flopping over the grass and shading it out.

The plan adds a pavilion in which to sit and admire the garden. Mrs Fish had little time for sitting, and her garden had the Bartram, a sort of barn which she used as a workshop, store and garden room. The plan here suggests a rustic shelter, based on one made by a friend of Mrs Fish's who grew many of her plants. This shelter was made in an afternoon from scrap from the sawmill, and it is relatively simple to imitate. Five upright poles are set into concrete bases; then the lintels and a pitched roof is nailed on. The roof is covered with bark offcuts lapped horizontally to make

The vigorous Gladiolus byzantinus *makes a brave show beneath the foliage of a hazel with dark red leaves. The opposite side of the path is dense with* Brunnera macrophylla, *whose sprays of blue flowers will cover the path in spring.*

Margery Fish's garden has a ditch running through it. Some gardeners would have tried to hide it, but it gave her an opportunity for yet more lovely plants. Here, Arum italicum 'Pictum', snowdrops, hellebores, crocuses and other bulbs make a pretty show in early spring.

a weathertight cover. The back walls are made of more horizontal bark planks, and give additional stability to the building as well as shelter to the occupant. The floor is of concrete with a circular pattern of stones embedded in it whilst the concrete is still soft.

No boundary is shown on the plan. At East Lambrook Manor, the garden is enclosed on two sides by the low retaining wall of the village lane. Elsewhere, rough hedging of quickthorn keeps out wind and grazing stock. However, fencing, picket fencing or chestnut palisading would be fine too.

PLANTING AND MAINTAINING IT

If the space where the flowers are to grow is presently under grass, lift 7cm/3in-thick turves from the area to be planted – this task is easily, if energetically, done with a standard spade. Compost the results, or build some turf seats, which can be surprisingly comfortable and long-lasting. A number of insect larvae feed beneath lawns, and may, if hungry, decide your herbaceous plants make a tolerable substitute. It is best to dig the area thoroughly, and let the birds clear away the larvae. If the lawn was filled with dandelions, creeping buttercup, couch grass and other deep-rooted things, leave the new area unplanted for a few months, then weedkill.

First to go in should be the row of clipped conifers. Use semi-mature plants, and the garden will swiftly take on a designed feel. If planting youngsters, leave the area around them unplanted for two seasons; otherwise the surrounding planting, vigorous and hungry, will overwhelm the young trees or shrubs if your back is turned for more than a week or two in summer. Mrs Fish used *Chamaecyparis lawsoniana* 'Fletcheri' for these. If you hate the idea of a Lawson's cypress in any form, I suggest you use one of the deep green juniper species.

For the trees, the plan suggests *Laburnum alpinum* at the far end of the garden. Though this species has small racemes, the flowers have an excellent smell, and if you grow the plant as a multistemmed tree, rather than as a formal standard, the plants soon look very picturesque, and eventually perfect for an added clematis or a rose. The double-flowered gean (*Prunus avium* 'Plena') can be a wonder in spring, its branches weighed down with the abundance of flowers. In gardens prone to late frosts, the crop can be killed if there's a hard freeze. Its leaves colour splendidly in autumn. Young trees sometimes need spraying against the blackfly that can infest new growth. Larger trees seem to build up a good population of aphid predators.

Of the witch hazels, the *Hamamelis* variety suggested here is *H.* x *intermedia* 'Pallida'. At least two plants seem to be in commerce under this name, both with pale daffodil yellow flowers. The best has an absolutely marvellous perfume that carries through the whole garden in February. The other has no discernible smell at all. If at all possible, buy your plants in flower so that you can check.

When buying containerized primulas, check for vine weevil grubs. Mature insects chew oblong notches from the leaf margins – the grubs will eat every last fragment of root, and even the crown of the plant as well. If your garden already has them, there's hardly any point in growing expensive named sorts of primula and polyanthus.

Margery Fish gardened in a mild part of Britain. In colder areas, some plants, particularly *Neillia thibetica,* are not always hardy. Even the lime-green-flowered *Euphorbia characias* subsp. *wulfenii* can be killed. As an insurance, root a few stalks of it indoors over winter – this is particularly easy to do, even in a jam jar of water.

Otherwise, watch for the thugs in the planting. *Macleaya cordata* usually has major ambitions. Unwanted stems are easily pulled out, but avoid the yellow sap that oozes from the wound. The plant is handsome in summer, and even more gorgeous in autumn.

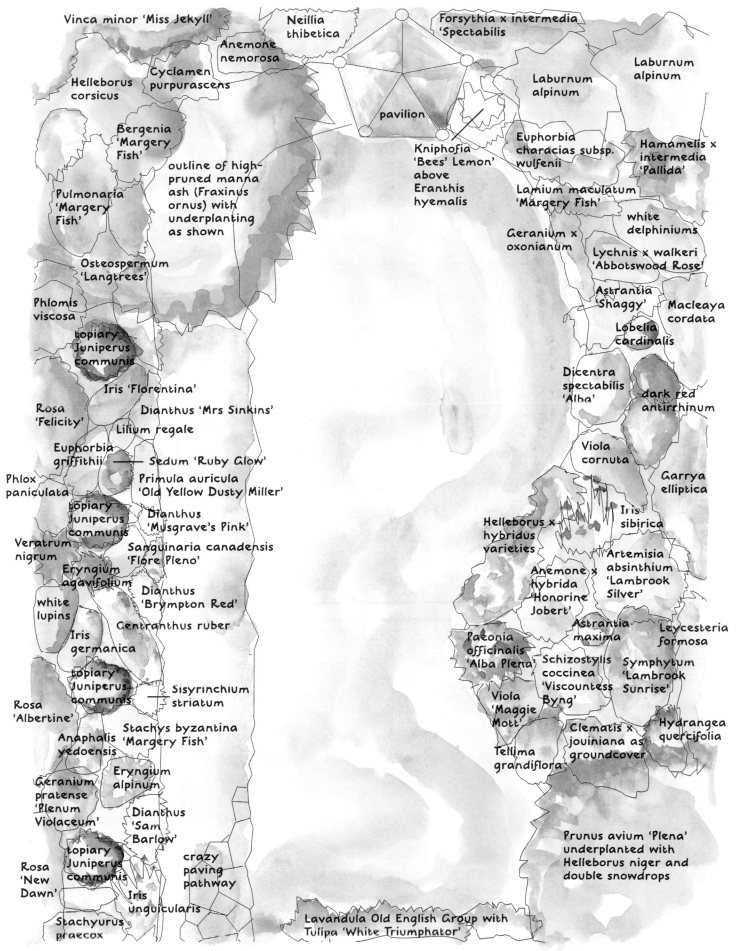

SHOPPING LIST

BULBS

12 *Cyclamen purpurascens*

50 *Eranthis hyemalis*

60 *Galanthus* (double snowdrops)

6 *Lilium regale*

50 *Tulipa* 'White Triumphator'

HERBACEOUS PLANTING

3 *Anaphalis margaritacea* var. *yedoensis*

5 *Anemone* x *hybrida* 'Honorine Jobert'

50 *Anemone nemorosa*

1 *Artemisia absinthium* 'Lambrook Silver'

3 *Astrantia major* subsp. *involucrata* 'Shaggy'

3 *Astrantia maxima*

6 *Bergenia* 'Margery Fish'

1 *Clematis* x *jouiniana*

6 *Delphinium*, white

1 *Dianthus* 'Brympton Red'

1 *Dianthus* 'Mrs Sinkins'

1 *Dianthus* 'Musgrave's Pink'

1 *Dianthus* 'Sam Barlow'

3 *Dicentra spectabilis* 'Alba'

3 *Eryngium agavifolium*

3 *Eryngium alpinum*

3 *Euphorbia characias* subsp. *wulfenii*

3 *Euphorbia griffithii*

3 *Geranium pratense* 'Plenum Violaceum'

8 *Geranium* x *oxonianum*

6 *Helleborus corsicus*

12 *Helleborus niger*

15 *Helleborus* x *hybridus* varieties

3 *Iris* 'Florentina'

3 *Iris germanica*

3 *Iris unguicularis*

3 *Kniphofia* 'Bees' Lemon'

6 *Lamium maculatum* 'Margery Fish'

12 *Lavandula* x *intermedia* Old English Group

3 *Leycesteria formosa*

3 *Lobelia cardinalis*

3 *Lychnis* x *walkeri* 'Abbotswood Rose'

3 *Macleaya cordata*

6 *Osteospermum jucundum* 'Langtrees'

3 *Paeonia officinalis* 'Alba Plena'

3 *Phlomis viscosa*

6 *Phlox paniculata*

3 *Primula auricula* 'Old Yellow Dusty Miller'

5 *Pulmonaria* 'Margery Fish'

3 *Sanguinaria canadensis* f. *multiplex* 'Plena'

6 *Schizostylis coccinea* 'Viscountess Byng'

3 *Sedum* 'Ruby Glow'

3 *Sisyrinchium striatum*

6 *Stachys byzantina* 'Margery Fish'

3 *Symphytum* 'Lambrook Sunrise'

6 *Tellima grandiflora*

3 *Veratrum nigrum*

12 *Vinca minor* 'Miss Jekyll'

12 *Viola cornuta*

6 *Viola* 'Maggie Mott'

ROSES

1 *Rosa* 'Albertine'

1 *Rosa* 'Felicity'

1 *Rosa* 'New Dawn'

SEED

12 *Antirrhinum*, dark red

25 *Centranthus ruber*

6 *Lupinus*, white

SHRUBS

3 *Forsythia* x *intermedia* 'Spectabilis'

3 *Garrya elliptica*

3 *Hamamelis* x *intermedia* 'Pallida'

1 *Hydrangea quercifolia*

4 *Juniperus communis*

1 *Neillia thibetica*

1 *Stachyurus praecox*

TREES

1 *Fraxinus ornus* (manna ash)

2 *Laburnum alpinum*

1 *Prunus avium* 'Plena'

Opposite left: *Garrya elliptica*
Opposite centre: *Dicentra spectabilis* 'Alba'
Opposite right: *Helleborus* x *hybridus*
Top right: *Hamamelis* x *intermedia* 'Pallida'
Centre right: *Astrantia major* subsp. *involucrata* 'Shaggy'
Bottom: *Euphorbia characias* subsp. *wulfenii*

THE PERFECT POTAGER

ROSEMARY VEREY AT BARNSLEY HOUSE

SOME BRITISH GARDENERS have an extraordinary talent for re-creating long-lost pasts, and delightful, if slightly fictitious, golden ages. So it was with Rosemary Verey and the re-creation of the potager. Although the word potager means, in its country of origin, merely a place for growing pot herbs or vegetables, without any thought of 'style', the word has come to mean, for many gardeners, a place where pretty flowers and tasty vegetables and fruit combine to make a charming whole.

The idea is not new. Modest mid-17th-century gardens, especially in the north of England and in Scotland, cheerfully combined honeysuckle and roses with cabbages and parsnips. And lovely books like John Reid's *The Scots Gardener* (1683) extol gardens in which the driving ideal was to get the maximum delight and nurture from the smallest space. Of course, it was easier in the past. Not only was labour very much cheaper, but also many plants we now think of as flowers – violets, pinks, lilies, roses, lavender, and so on – were once intensely useful and often had now-vanished roles in the kitchen, as well as their more usual functions in cosmetics and as remedies for illness. This usefulness didn't stop gardeners also rejoicing in their colours and perfumes while the plants were still in the garden. In the 17th century, too, the appreciation of all sorts of plants was higher, and the segregation of vegetables and fruits into some humbler garden category than shrubs and flowers had not yet taken place.

Reid's sort of garden sounds lovely, and in part of the garden at Barnsley House in Gloucestershire, the late Rosemary Verey, beginning in the 1960s, made an enchanting similar mix, using modern as well as ancient varieties. Her potager garden entirely meets the old criteria of usefulness and delight. Small-scaled and very simply put together, it is also extremely adaptable, which makes it a suitable way of gardening in smaller spaces. It also makes a fulfilling garden, even if it is the only one you have room for.

NOTES ON THE PLAN

Apart from the need to keep caterpillars off the cabbages, and similar chores, the only other slight problem is that whatever you harvest for the kitchen almost always leaves bare soil, until new seedlings of another crop begin to make a show. The garden also needs fairly constant work, though the rewards are correspondingly high. It is lovely to take a bunch of pinks

Box-edged beds filled with pink and purple lavender and the abundantly flowering rose 'White Pet', grown as standards, make a colourful and highly decorative centrepiece to Rosemary Verey's vegetable garden at Barnsley House.

whilst harvesting a salad for lunch, and fun to smell the lavender whilst weeding the runner beans.

The garden needs to get plenty of sun, and won't do well if shady, though some salad crops will still yield well. The site's soil isn't that important; you can build up good fertile soil over five or six seasons, if you have room for composting the splendid amounts of kitchen waste that this garden produces. It is even possible to make a potager on a hard site, using raised beds in a parterre plan. I grow excellent beans, squashes and salads on a stone and concrete floor of an old roofless byre. The beds have a 45cm/18in depth of compost.

BUILDING IT

An important element in the Barnsley House potager is a lovely variant of the fruit or laburnum tunnel often found in country house gardens. Here, the arching metal struts are often planted with a mix of scarlet runner beans and one of the yellow courgettes (many non-bush marrows, squashes and so on climb vigorously if allowed). When the whole lot's in fruit, the effect is sumptuous. There are many suppliers of suitable arches, and even some of garden tunnels, though a generously scaled pergola of wooden poles would be quite as effective. In the plan, the tunnel is shown making an arbour for a couple of seats, and the width of the tunnel needs to accommodate them. It would also be possible to use the tunnel as a cage for soft fruit (strawberries, blackcurrants, gooseberries,

Far left: Many marrow and squash varieties will climb enthusiastically, and at Barnsley ripening marrows hang heavily from the arches. Tall sunflowers add colour above, as well as seeds for the birds, while below, yet another American plant, Rudbeckia hirta 'Marmalade', edges the simple brick and concrete path.

Left: Different sorts of vegetables, or visually different sorts of the same vegetable species, can be combined to make intriguing patterns; here, sweetcorn and a red-leaved lettuce create a flamboyant planting.

and so on), by covering it with suitable netting. Black is the best colour. Runner or climbing French beans would cheerfully grow up the outside, to provide some greenery and colour, though they would need to be widely spaced to avoid shading out the fruit beneath.

The Barnsley House potager tunnel is at its best from late June or so, but to provide earlier colour, the strips of soil along the tunnel's feet are planted up with *Rudbeckia hirta* 'Marmalade' (sown early under glass), and giant sunflowers. It works marvellously, but you might like the more culinary marigold, *Calendula officinalis* ('Art Shades' is a splendid mix of silvery yellows and burnt orange), which Mrs Verey also used.

The other important building work lies in the paths. A potager always involves digging and muddy shoes. Brick is the best surface (gravel often ends up inside the house), ideally frost-proof engineering bricks laid in herringbone or basket-weave pattern. At Barnsley House, the paths incorporate bricks, concrete slabs, stone and more. They constitute one of the decorative elements of the garden.

The plan assumes a fenced boundary, either of planking or chestnut staves. It also assumes that the fencing is around 1.5m/5ft high, and will support planting, perhaps alternating cordons of gooseberries and redcurrants (gooseberries are often left alone by predators until they are ripe enough for you to want them too) or a mix of roses and cordon apples.

PLANTING AND MAINTAINING IT

Once the paths are in place, plant the box. If you have access to a mature bush, or another hedge, in early spring or mid-autumn sink 15cm/6in sprigs two-thirds of their length into the soil, a sprig every 15cm/6in. Most will root with ease. If you buy in young plants, spacing depends on their size, and on your patience. Plants in 10cm/4in pots could be spaced every 23cm/9in apart. The planting will make a closed edge in the third season. Box is a greedy feeder, and will mine nutrients from your composted vegetable beds. The roots need severing with a spade just beyond the margin of the edging every second season or so.

The plan doesn't specify the varieties of fruit, though the shopping list makes suggestions for the trees giving central emphasis to some of the beds. Apples are best grown on dwarfing stock to keep them small. If you enjoy pruning, pears can be kept to some very decorative shapes. In a small potager, standard-trained soft fruit, like redcurrants or red- or yellow-fruited gooseberries, can look extremely pretty.

How the vegetable and salad beds are planted is up to you. The Barnsley House potager makes use of decorative varieties of cabbages and some kales, broccolis, chicories, chards and other beet crops, lettuces and leeks (there are some splendid purple-foliaged forms). Other low-growing crops are also ideal: radishes, French beans, rocket, chervil, cresses and more. Chards, leeks and some of the chicories will give a touch of colour for some of the winter. Any lamb's lettuce left over from an autumn sowing gives tiny blue flowers in early spring. There are very few annual fruits. Most useful, if you have a warm garden, are some of the Chinese lantern (*Physalis*) species.

Tall-growing crops like Brussels sprouts, most sprouting broccolis and sweetcorn could be grown in the side beds beneath the cordon fruits. Most potatoes are too exuberant for such highly designed spaces, though I'd make an exception for one of the delicious purple-fleshed and purple-flowered varieties such as 'Peruvian Purple Fingerling'.

Although it would be possible to assign the beds to a strict rotational system used in serious vegetable gardening, here it is only important to keep the soil producing something attractive to look at and to eat.

The central herb garden is always going to be at least a little untidy. Grow the mints in elderly leaky buckets sunk to their rims in the bed; that will stop the mint runners taking over the entire space. The balm will flop happily, and the tarragon will need the sort of support usually given to herbaceous flowers. The rosemary obelisks at the start of the garden, once established, can be pruned twice a year. The variety suggested has fairly typical blue flowers. The white-flowered variety also clips well.

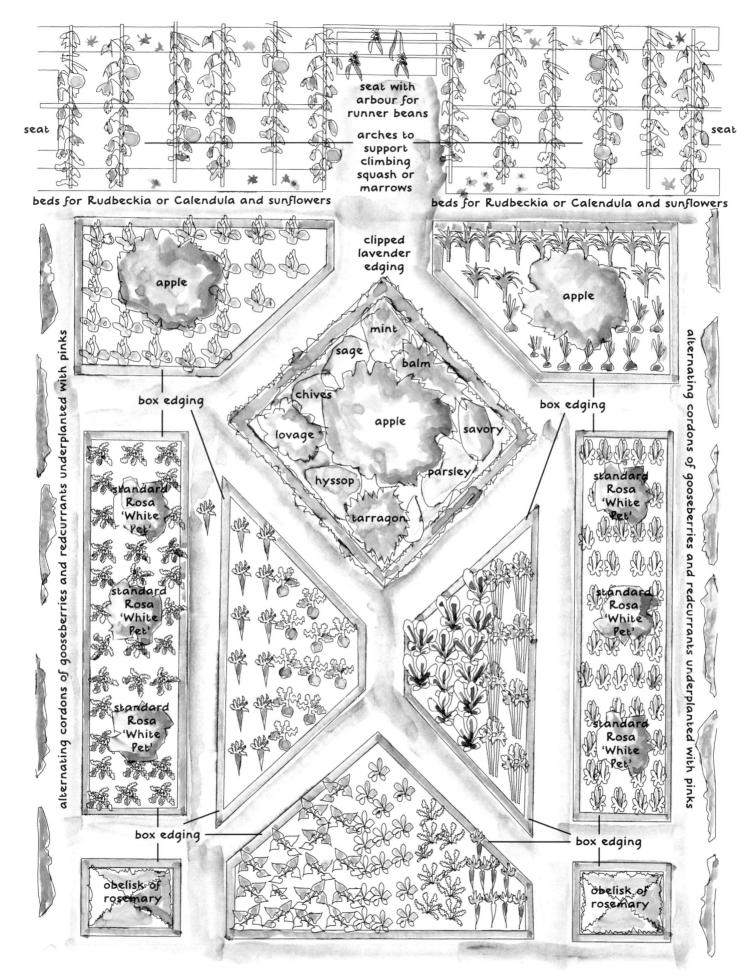

seat with arbour for runner beans

arches to support climbing squash or marrows

seat

seat

beds for Rudbeckia or Calendula and sunflowers

beds for Rudbeckia or Calendula and sunflowers

clipped lavender edging

apple

apple

box edging

box edging

mint

sage

balm

chives

lovage

apple

savory

parsley

hyssop

tarragon

alternating cordons of gooseberries and redcurrants underplanted with pinks

alternating cordons of gooseberries and redcurrants underplanted with pinks

standard Rosa 'White Pet'

standard Rosa 'White Pet'

standard Rosa 'White Pet'

standard Rosa 'White Pet'

standard Rosa 'White Pet'

standard Rosa 'White Pet'

box edging

box edging

obelisk of rosemary

obelisk of rosemary

SHOPPING LIST

FRUITS

1 apple 'Cox's Orange Pippin'

1apple 'Newton Wonder'

1 apple 'Ashmead's Kernel'

6 redcurrant cordons

6 gooseberry cordons

SHRUBS

600 *Buxus sempervirens* (box)

40 *Lavendula angustifolia* 'Hidcote Pink' (lavender)

12 *Rosmarinus officinalis* 'Miss Jessop's Upright' (rosemary)

3 *Salvia officinalis* (sage)

HERBACEOUS PLANTING

3 *Allium schoenoprasum* (chives)

3 *Artemisia dracunculus* 'Sativa' (French tarragon)

12 *Dianthus* 'Loveliness' (pinks)

3 *Melissa officinalis* (balm)

3 *Mentha* species (mint)

3 *Satureja officinalis* (savory)

ROSES

6 *Rosa* 'White Pet' standards

SEED

Calendula officinalis (marigolds)

carrot

celery, red-leaved

cos lettuce

Helianthus 'Vanilla Ice' or 'Italian White' (sunflowers)

hyssop

leek

lettuce, oak-leaved green

lettuce, oak-leaved red

lovage

onion

parsley

raddichio

radish

Rudbeckia hirta 'Marmalade'

runner beans 'Sunset'

spinach

squash or non-bush marrows

Swiss chard, 'Rhubarb Chard'

Opposite above: *Calendula* 'Art Shades'
Opposite below: 'Rhubarb Chard'
Top left: Mint
Top centre: Variegated balm
Top right: Chives in flower
Bottom left: *Rudbeckia hirta* 'Marmalade'
Bottom right: Radishes

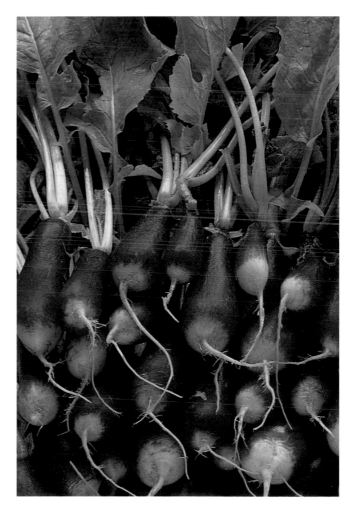

THE ARTFUL ORCHARD

MIRIAM ROTHSCHILD AT ASHTON WOLD

T HIS, the simplest of all the plans, and ultimately an extremely satisfying garden, is one of the more difficult to achieve. All gardening is artifice in some degree, and though this lovely orchard looks as if it is a 'natural' piece of untouched meadow, it is in fact as carefully worked out, and as carefully planned, as any in this book.

At Ashton Wold, in Northamptonshire, the eminent naturalist and wildflower-enthusiast Dame Miriam Rothschild started with an established orchard, largely of apple trees, and a romantic thatched summerhouse from which to view it. A gnarled but vigorous apple tree, half-hidden by its flowers, is one of the most marvellous sights of spring. If it has a prosperous season, it becomes marvellous once more in autumn, branches weighted with fruit. Pears can be perhaps even more exciting in spring, as can plums, peaches and apricots, but nothing beats an apple in autumn, as the leaves turn sere and the fruits begin to colour.

NOTES ON THE PLAN

In this plan, unlike the others, where fruit varieties have not been specified, varieties that would have been grown at Ashton Wold are listed. All are delicious, from the waxen and tiny 'Yellow Ingestre' that in September tastes of champagne to the sumptuously flavoured, long-keeping 'Margil' of the following March and April. If these are not the old varieties of your region, try to plant ones that are. The popular named sorts sold at most garden centres are usually bred for commerce, and give little hint of the subtleties of flavour, texture and visual delight of which apples are capable.

BUILDING IT

The only man-made structure is some sort of focal point, ideally a summerhouse as rustic as you can make it. The one at Ashton Wold is of timber, and thatched. An off-the-shelf one will need to be painted a dark colour, and covered as quickly as possible with ivy and roses. The rose

A simple mown path gives access through the meadow, the long grass rich with daffodils and a scattering of Leucojum aestivum. *The apple trees are left to grow as they please, flower prodigiously in spring and yield beautifully in autumn.*

Far left: The meadow planting in spring has natives, like cowslips (Primula veris) and bluebells (Hycacinthoides non-scripta), as well as more exotic plants like the poet's narcissus (Narcissus poeticus) and a commercial variety of tulip. The thatched hut makes a perfect excuse to explore.

Left: Later in summer, cow parsley (Anthriscus sylvestris), with its lovely perfume, sweet cicely (Myrrhis odorata) and other umbellifers are in full flower, covering up the spent flowers of earlier in the season. The young apples are beginning to swell, and some will soon be ready for the table.

suggested here ('Paul's Himalayan Musk') is tough and extremely vigorous, with huge amounts of pale amethyst flowers. Alternatively, cover it with a clematis or two – a mix of *Clematis macropetala* and *C.* 'Kermesina' is vigorous and colourful without being too showy.

Some companies sell small buildings which are summerhouses at the front and storage sheds behind – an ideal arrangement, especially as the garden will need frost-free storage for the 'keeping' varieties of fruit. The summerhouse will make a perfect place to sample them as they ripen, and, once winter is past, watch the orchard come back into flower.

PLANTING IT

The most difficult 'building' work is clearing the ground. Ideally, the flowers that will spangle the grass beneath the trees need to be planted in clean ground. They also need to be pre-grown. At Ashton Wold, there are extensive ranges of glasshouses devoted to raising young primulas, cowslips, fritillaries, campions and so on. The more showy bulbs, tulips, narcissus and colchicums, can be bought in, but even these will establish very much better if planted so that they do not, in the first season or two, have to compete with a cover of grass. If the area that you are going to use is already grassland, skim it all off and use the turves elsewhere, or compost them. Alternatively, use a weedkiller, though with great care. Many, even those not supposed to leave residues, can have more long-lasting effects than their manufacturers claim. At the very least, strip patches of turf away from the areas where you intend to have wildflowers. It is tempting to simply clear the ground and sow one of the 'meadow mixtures' promoted in seed catalogues. These can look quite pretty, but check exactly what species they contain. They probably have some you would not consider 'wild' in your locality. They are also often temporary; the grass species are vigorous enough to stop the annual flowers becoming established, and you will end up after a season or two with undecorated grassland.

Start off the perennial flowers you want to establish from seed as soon as possible, and get them lined out in the open ground if there's not time or space to grow them in individual pots as at Ashton Wold. When planting them in their final locations, arrange them in groups of six and seven. The primula species look good clustered around the tree trunks, and will also benefit from the composting the trees will receive.

Sow grass seed either in the autumn following the spring planting-out of bulbs and perennial wildflowers, or the following spring. Once the seed is broadcast, sow irregular patches of the annual wildflowers.

The young trees also need no competition in their first few seasons. When buying, check what variety forms the rootstock. Many garden centres sell material grafted on strongly dwarfing stock, assuming that most of their customers want small and early-cropping trees. Such plants will not make a convincing orchard, so look for ones grafted on medium or non-dwarfing stocks. Check that the range of varieties you have will enable plenty of cross-pollination. The varieties suggested will be fine, but if you plant local varieties, check pollination needs with your supplier.

The plan does not propose filbert varieties. These, in any case, vary from place to place. The only important consideration is to plant at least two varieties if you want a good crop (fresh filberts, still a bit green, are more delicious than the dry ones eaten at Christmas). If you want to hedge the garden off from the world, buy more of the eglantines (*Rosa rubiginosa*). The species makes an excellent and dense thorny hedge, the young leaves of spring smell of apple pie (especially strong after a shower), the pink flowers are abundant and the garnet-red fruit will feed your birds well into winter.

Once established the whole planting will give something nice from earliest spring well into high summer. Autumn will be good too; fallen russet apples and a purple colchicum like *Colchicum speciosum*, or the easy-to-grow double 'Waterlily', make a very smart ensemble.

MAINTAINING IT

After five or six seasons, the fruit trees will be making good growth, and some shaping will be needed. After that, they can be left alone. Garden manuals make much of pruning – fine if you want to maximize the crop, and want perfect fruit. An established orchard, even unpruned and unsprayed, will give such gluts of fruit that your friends and even your hungry wildlife will be dismayed.

The grassland is more problematic. Natural meadows survive as a mix of grasses and flowers because the soil is low in nutrients, and the vigorous grasses cannot dominate everything else. Meadows are also grazed. The grass path to the summerhouse will need to be mown as a normal lawn. The 'artful' areas will need to be cut around six weeks after the narcissus have finished flowering. The area will look unpleasant for the succeeding fortnight, by which time it will start greening up again. Leave the summer-flowering area until August or so. The hay needs to be removed and composted elsewhere. If left *in situ* it will add nutrients to the meadow, giving grass the upper hand in the struggle for survival.

Keep a watch for perennial weeds. Docks (*Rumex* species) can look good as their seed heads mature to wonderful earthy reds, but weedkill in spring if you end up with too many. The creeping thistle (*Cirsium arvense*), though a food crop for some handsome butterflies, should be watched carefully. It can easily take over whole areas of garden. Nettles (*Urtica dioica*) will also invade. Nettle soup is not especially good, and a vigorous clump cheerfully shades out anything it grows over. Kill.

Urban gardeners often love the idea of an orchard, but fear that it will merely attract thieves. However, most children have a limited knowledge of gardening and cooking, and anyway usually steal apples long before the fruit is ripe. Plant fruits they know nothing of – quinces, mulberries, myrobalans, damsons, crabs, and many more nuts. Medlars are wonderful in flower and in autumn, though the fruit hardly justifies more than a single tree.

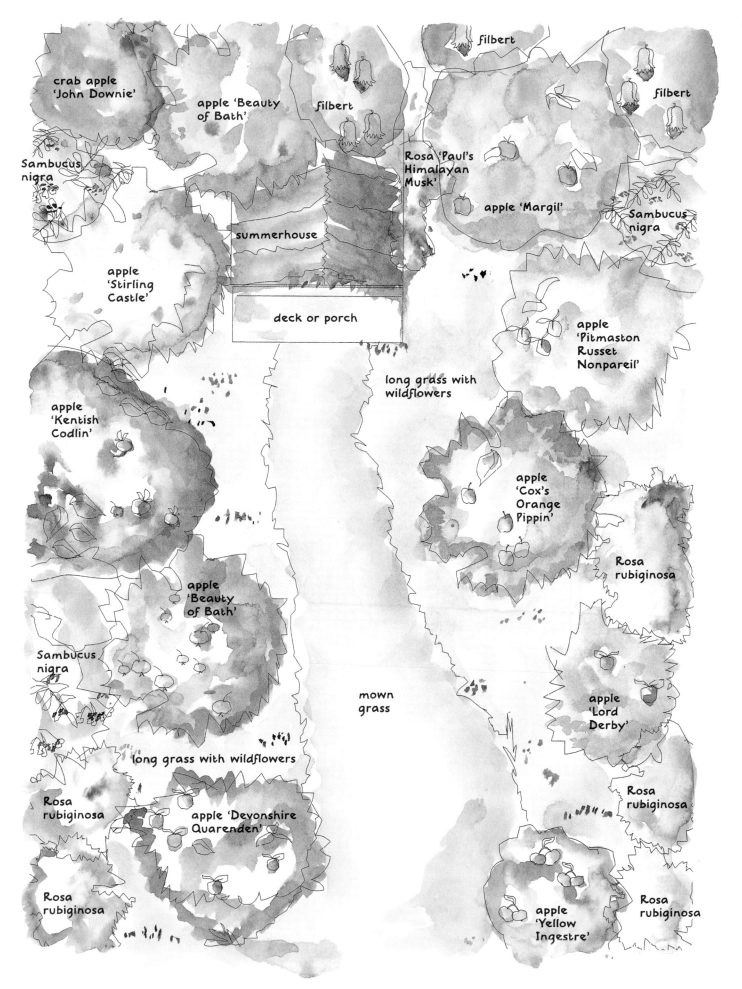

crab apple 'John Downie'

apple 'Beauty of Bath'

filbert

filbert

Sambucus nigra

Rosa 'Paul's Himalayan Musk'

apple 'Margil'

filbert

Sambucus nigra

summerhouse

apple 'Stirling Castle'

deck or porch

apple 'Pitmaston Russet Nonpareil'

long grass with wildflowers

apple 'Kentish Codlin'

apple 'Cox's Orange Pippin'

Rosa rubiginosa

apple 'Beauty of Bath'

Sambucus nigra

mown grass

apple 'Lord Derby'

long grass with wildflowers

Rosa rubiginosa

Rosa rubiginosa

apple 'Devonshire Quarenden'

Rosa rubiginosa

apple 'Yellow Ingestre'

Rosa rubiginosa

SHOPPING LIST

BULBS

100 *Camassia leichtlinii*

100 *Leucojum aestivum*

100 *Narcissus* 'Cheerfulness'

100 *Tulipa* 'Peach Blossom'

HERBACEOUS PLANTING

50 *Centaurea montana* (perennial cornflower)

10 *Geranium pratense* (field geranium)

50 *Lychnis flos-cuculi* (ragged Robin) **X**

50 *Myrrhis odorata* (sweet cicely) **X**

50 *Silene dioica* (red campion) **X**

(those marked **X** are also easily grown from seed)

SEED

(Sow when sowing grass seed in the autumn of the garden's second season)

Agrostemma githago (corncockle)

Leucanthemum vulgare (ox-eye daisy)

Papaver rhoeas (corn poppy)

ROSES

15 *Rosa rubiginosa* (eglantine)

1 *Rosa* 'Paul's Himalayan Musk'

TREES

2 apple ''Beauty of Bath'

1 apple 'Cox's Orange Pippin'

1 apple 'Devonshire Quarenden'

1 apple 'Kentish Codlin'

1 apple 'Lord Derby'

1 apple 'Margil'

1 apple 'Pitmaston Russet Nonpareil'

1 apple 'Stirling Castle'

1 apple 'Yellow Ingestre'

1 *Malus* 'John Downie' (crab apple)

3 filbert

3 *Sambucus nigra*

NOTE ON PLANTING

The view from the summerhouse may include your own living quarters. The garden front of Ashton Wold is liberally hung with a huge wisteria, perhaps a nice idea for decorating your own.

Opposite above: *Malus* 'John Downie'
Opposite below: apple 'Cox's Orange Pippin'
Above left: *Rosa rubiginosa*
Above right: *Silene dioica*
Centre: *Papaver rhoeas*
Below left: *Agrostemma githago*
Below right: *Leucanthemum vulgare*

THE SUNSET PRAIRIE

PIET OUDOLF AT HUMMELO

MOST OF THE classic garden plans in this book look back, in one way or another, to the past. Contemporary classics are harder to find. Some designers experiment with coloured polycarbonate sheets instead of hedges or formal layouts of bagels instead of parterres, or make abstract landscapes of grass and water, or use mist machines to turn gardens into instant rain forests. However, new classics are more likely to be found where a designer puts plants, perhaps new or neglected plant groups, together in new ways, as, for example, 19th-century gardeners did when they discovered ferns and made fern gardens.

Recently, a group of late-20th-century gardener-designers have turned to grasses and sedges, treating them in a new way – though one that is similar to Gertrude Jekyll's (at the time) innovative planting of flowers such as delphiniums, lupins and so on in large groups and drifts. The new designers have also added grassland flowers, notably some of the wonders from the prairies of the United States – rudbeckias, milkweeds, monardas and the like.

The popularity of new garden styles has often been affected by advances in media technology – illustration reproduction, the advent of photography and so on – and this new style is no exception. The arrival of inexpensive high quality colour printing has created a new need for arresting images and an interest in fleeting garden moments, especially at previously unphotographed times of day. Flowering grasses look most spectacular when oblique light catches the architecture of their flowering stems. The reddish golden light of a summer sunset is especially good: the colour washes over the whole flower border, uniting the colours in subtle ways once much used by painters. Blues, purples and reds all become sumptuously vibrant, and the low sunlight catches the complex structure of grass panicles and makes the narrowest of stems glow with light.

Dense plantings of geraniums, salvias, grasses, eryngiums and monardas almost swamp this path through Piet Oudolf's garden at Hummelo in the Netherlands. The warm colour range here works perfectly in high sunlight, but looks sensational when washed with the golden glow of a summer evening.

The new designers began to create and photograph some extremely impressive plantings, ones that could be used as convincingly in large public spaces as in small domestic areas. One of the most creative of the group is Piet Oudolf, who has an international reputation as a designer, a fine nursery in his native Holland, an observant camera and a handsome private garden. The plan here makes use of many of his most cherished plants, and puts them together in a similar way. The layout and a design element or two come from his garden at Hummelo in the Netherlands.

Opposite: Echinaceas, monardas and a grass for contrast, all easily grown and easily maintained, make a harmonious mix that would work perfectly in almost any garden.

Below: Hedges, though they make work, are important in giving structure to informal plantings, and can also be enormous fun. Here, gently undulating and folded hedges make a handsome and very theatrical backdrop to an autumnal planting.

Veronicastrums, phlox, eupatoriums and the flower spikes of lysimachias, with their contrasting forms and already complementary colours, are turned into a sumptuous tapestry by the evening light, at a time of day when many gardeners can at last relax and enjoy their borders.

His designs have a strong architectural style, often allied with amusing and quirky detailing. He also has immense taste in combining plants, and using interesting ones. Though clearly a design descendant of William Robinson and Gertrude Jekyll, using single-species clumps in the Jekyll manner, and as clever with colour and texture as she, he could be said to be designing for a new season and a new time of day — late summer and late in the day. Because of changing times, his borders are not tidied away in early autumn; labour is now expensive. But this gives the borders a second season, when hoar frost emphasizes the structure of stems and dead leaves, and makes the airy engineering of the grasses a wonder to behold.

NOTES ON THE PLAN
The circular raised bed and its asymmetrical approach are based on some of the design elements at Hummelo. The aspen trees add height and the cool silvery glitter of their leaves, a good foil for the rich colours in the rest of the garden.

The garden's flowering season runs from June into November, but does not really include spring. If you can forgo some of the decorative effects provided by the hoar frosts of spring, strim the dead vegetation down in January, and have a huge early spring flowering of the lovely pale violet *Crocus tommasinianus*, with its brilliantly orange styles. The crocus actually does best among herbaceous plants, needing the disturbance of their replanting cycle to break up the dense clusters of bulbs that soon form and, being cramped, stop flowering.

BUILDING IT
Check the orientation of your garden to see if the low summer evening sun reaches where you plan to have the border, so that the light will flood over the plants without shining straight into the eyes of the onlooker.

There are some ingenious path designs at Hummelo, using a great range of materials. For this path, use brick paviours to outline groups of four stone or concrete paving slabs. The raised bed needs a brick retaining wall with a brick coping. The coping is intended as an additional seating area from which to view the sumptuous colours of the flowers, so the overall height should be about 40cm/16in. The seats themselves should be wood, solid and comfortable, somewhere good to watch the light fading over the rudbeckias and salvias and grasses, or to see the sunlight of a winter day catching the ice on the frilled and spiny heads of eryngiums.

PLANTING AND MAINTAINING IT
The hedge plants need to go in during the garden's building phase, to give both shelter and a frame to the planting as soon as possible. The trees can wait for a season or two. If you find the thought of planting aspens alarming, then plant rowans for the birds. They will have all the seed from the border to eat, but rowan berries would be good too. Most rowans have an attractive show of fruit in autumn, and some, like *Sorbus vilmorinii*, have lacquered scarlet foliage too.

Getting in the herbaceous planting is straightforward. For the first season or two there will be little work except for weeding. Strim down the herbaceous straw in late January or February, as plants begin to grow again. Some of the evergreen grasses will also need their foliage renewed if it is looking tired. Strim those too. Rake off the mess and compost the results, to be spread over the border in a season or two.

Some of the plants are invasive, and will swamp lesser ones. Keep grasses, lysimachia and persicaria in check, though a certain tangle will give a much more naturalistic effect, even though long-term maintenance of the border will become difficult when you need to separate and renew the clumps. Creeping thistle, nettle and buttercups will also invade if they can. The last two usually remain with some foliage over winter, and start growing early. Spray new growth with a systemic herbicide, which will usually control them. Keep the spray away from evergreen grasses.

SHOPPING LIST

GRASSES/SEDGES

3 *Calamagrostis brachytricha*

6 *Chionochloa rubra*

6 *Cortaderia selloana* 'Pumila'

3 *Helictotrichon sempervirens*

3 *Miscanthus sinensis* 'Kleine Fontäne'

3 *Miscanthus sinensis* 'Kleine Silberspinne'

6 *Molinina caerulea* subsp. *arundinacea*

15 *Pennisetum villosum*

9 *Sesleria caerulea*

1 *Stipa gigantea*

HERBACEOUS PLANTING

3 *Actaea racemosa* (syn. *Cimicifuga racemosa*)

12 *Ajuga reptans*

6 *Ajuga reptans* 'Atropurpurea'

4 *Astilbe* 'Europa'

3 *Astilbe* x *arendsii* 'Spinell'

6 *Astrantia major* 'Rubra'

15 *Echinacea purpurea* 'Rubinstern'

6 *Eryngium planum*

6 *Eupatorium purpureum* subsp. *maculatum* 'Atropurpureum'

6 *Foeniculum vulgare* 'Purpureum'

8 *Hedera helix* 'Bowles Ox Heart'

6 *Helenium* 'Moerheim Beauty'

3 *Inula magnifica*

6 *Lobelia* 'Queen Victoria'

3 *Luzula sylvatica* 'Aurea'

6 *Luzula sylvatica* 'Marginata'

6 *Lychnis coronaria*

6 *Lysimachia atropurpurea*

3 *Lysimachia ephemerum*

6 *Lythrum salicaria*

6 *Monarda austromontana*

6 *Monarda* 'Cambridge Scarlet'

6 *Monarda* 'Croftway Pink'

12 *Omphalodes verna*

3 *Persicaria polymorpha*

6 *Phlomis russeliana*

1 *Phormium tenax*

6 *Rudbeckia fulgida* var. *sallivantii* 'Goldsturm'

9 *Salvia farinacea* 'Victoria'

6 *Salvia pratensis* Haematodes Group

3 *Salvia involucrata*

5 *Salvia* x 'Superba'

3 *Salvia verticillata* 'Purple Rain'

3 *Sanguisorba officinalis*

9 *Veronica longifolia*

6 *Veronicastrum virginicum*

SHRUBS AND TREES

1 *Buddleja davidii* 'Black Knight'

3 *Ceratostigma willmottianum*

50 *Ligustrum ovalifolium* (privet)

2 *Sorbaria kirilowii* (syn. *Spiraea arborea*)

50 *Taxus baccata* (yew)

2 *Populus tremula* (aspen)

Opposite: *Miscanthus sinensis* 'Kleine Fontäne'
Left: *Salvia verticillata* 'Purple Rain'
Above: *Stipa gigantea*
Right: *Phlomis russeliana*
Below left: *Helenium* 'Moerheim Beauty'
Below right: *Veronicastrum virginicum*

BIBLIOGRAPHY

Abbott, M. *Gardens of Plenty: The Art of the Potager Garden* 2001

Berthier, F. *Reading Zen in the Rocks: The Japanese Dry Landscape Garden* 2000

Brown, J. *Sissinghurst: Portrait of a Garden* 1990

Bultitude, J. *Apples; a Guide to Identification* 1984

Chivers, S. & Woloszynska, S. *The Cottage Garden: Margery Fish at East Lambrook Manor* 1990

Clarke, E. *Hidcote; the Making of a Garden* 1989

Brenzel, K. N. (ed) *Western Garden Book* 2001

Fish, M. *An All Year Round Garden* 1976

Gerritsen, H. & Oudolf, P. *Dream Plants for the Natural Garden* 2000

Gunter, N. *Japanese Gardens* 2003

Hadfield, M. (ed) *British Gardeners; a Biographical Dictionary* 1980

Hunt, J. *The Dutch Garden in the Seventeenth Century* 1990

Jacques, D. & van der Horst, J. *The Gardens of William and Mary* 1988

Jekyll, G. *Colour Schemes for the Flower Garden* 1908

Kawaguchi, Y. *Serene Gardens: Creating Japanese Design and Detail in the Western Garden* 2000

Keane, M. *Japanese Garden Design* 1997

Keswick, M. *The Chinese Garden: History, Art and Architecture* 1978

Larkcom, J. *Creative Vegetable Gardening* 2004

Lewis, P. *Making a Wildflower Meadow* 2003

Lockwood, A. (ed) *Gardens of Colony and State: Gardens and Gardeners of the American Colonies and of the Republic Before 1840* 2000

Massingham B. *Miss Jekyll: Portrait of a Great Gardener* 1973

Mcguire, D. (ed) *Horticulture: American Garden Design: An Anthology of Ideas That Shaped Our Landscape* 1994

Moynihan, E. *Paradise As a Garden: In Persia and Mughal India* 1979

Moynihan, E. *The Moonlight Garden: New Discoveries at the Taj Mahal* 2001

Nan Chung Wah *Art of Chinese Gardens* 1983

Olson, D. *Paradise Gardens* 1989

Oudolf, P. *Planting the Natural Garden* 2003

Plumptre, G. *The Water Garden* 1993

Recht, C. & Wetterwald M. *Bamboos* 1992

Rothschild, M. *The Rothschild Gardens* 1988

Streatfield, D. *California Gardens* 1994

Tankard, J. & Valkenburgh, M. *Gertrude Jekyll; a Vision of Garden and Wood* 1988

Tun-chen Liu, et al *Chinese Classical Gardens of Suzhou* 1993

Verey, R. *Rosemary Verey's Making of a Garden* 2001

Vertrees, J. D. *Japanese Maples* 1991

Walcott, M. V. *Wildflowers of America*

Wescoat, J. & Wolschke-Bulmahn, J. *Mughal Gardens: Sources, Places, Representations, and Prospects* 1996

PHOTOGRAPHIC ACKNOWLEDGMENTS

The Publishers have made every effort to contact holders of copyright works. Any copyright holders we have been unable to reach are invited to contact the Publishers so that a full acknowledgment may be given in subsequent editions. For permission to reproduce the images on the following pages and for supplying photographs, the Publishers thank those listed below.

(a = above, b = below, c = centre, l = left, r = right)

Art Directors & TRIP Photo Library: 32
© **David Austin Roses Limited:** 75al, 114a
Marc Auth/AUTH Photo: 35
© **Philippe Faucon (www.desert-tropicals.com):** 99ar, 99cr
Derek Fell: 50–51
John Glover: 5, 13, 22b, 23, 30, 31al, 31ac, 31bl, 31br, 39al, 39ar, 39bl, 39br, 49al, 49ac, 49ar, 49br, 56, 57al, 57ar, 57cr, 57bl, 66, 67al, 67ac, 67ar, 67c, 67cr, 67b, 68, 74, 75ar, 75bl, 75bc, 75br, 90a, 91ac, 91bl, 91bc, 91br, 98, 99bl, 107ac, 107ar, 107br, 115ar, 115br, 124, 125b, 132b, 133al, 133ar, 133bl, 133br, 140, 141ar, 141c, 141bl, 141br, 150, 151
Courtesy of Gravetye Manor (www.gravetyemanor.co.uk): 8, 60l, 60–61
Jerry Harpur: 11 (The Master of the Fishing Nets, Suzhou), 14–15 (The Master of the Fishing Nets, Suzhou), 16 (The Master of the Fishing Nets, Suzhou), 59 (Gravetye Manor), 100 (Hidcote Manor), 116 (East Lambrook Manor), 146–7 (designer Piet Oudolf, Hummelo, The Netherlands)
Sunniva Harte: 62–3
Peter Hayden: 17, 18
Marijke Heuff: 40, 145 (designer Piet Oudolf, Hummelo, The Netherlands)
Michèle Lamontagne: 24, 26, 27
Hugo Latymer: 48r
Andrew Lawson: 42–3 (Het Loo Palace, The Netherlands); 106b, 128–9 (Barnsley House, Gloucestershire), 134–5 (Ashton Wold, Northamptonshire), 136–7 (Ashton Wold, Northamptonshire), 144 (designer Piet Oudolf, Hummelo, The Netherlands)
Andrew Lawson © Frances Lincoln Limited: 39ac, 39cl, 57cl, 57c, 83, 91al, 91ar, 91cl, 91c, 91cr, 99ac, 99br, 107bl, 115l, 133ac, 141al
Tony Lord: 1, 44–5, 102, 103, 108, 110, 111, 126
Clive Nichols: 57br, 118–119, 120–1, 142–3 (designer Piet Oudolf, Hummelo, The Netherlands)
Private Collection: 70, 71
Royal Botanic Gardens, Edinburgh: 22a (photo L. A. Lavener)
Vivian Russell: 76–7, 79r
© **Stapeley Water Gardens Limited, UK:** 39cr, 82
Thompson & Morgan (UK) Limited: 38, 132a
Tim Street-Porter: 92, 94–5
David Stuart: 31ar, 45r, 48l, 49bl, 67cl, 90b, 99al, 106a, 107al, 114b, 115ac, 125a, 125c, 136l
Steven Wooster: 2–3, 6–7, 78–9, 84–5, 86, 87

PUBLISHERS' ACKNOWLEDGMENTS

Project editor: Sarah Mitchell
Designed by Anne Wilson
Picture editor: Sue Gladstone
Picture assistant: Milena Michalski
Index by Valerie Chandler
Production: Caterina Favaretto